Freed for Ever

Freed for Ever

a sequel to Freed for Life

Rita Nightingale

with David Porter

Marshalls

Marshalls Paperbacks
Marshall Morgan & Scott
3 Beggarwood Lane, Basingstoke, Hants, RG23 7LP, UK.

First published by Marshall Morgan & Scott 1985

British Library CIP data

Nightingale, Rita
  Freed forever.
  1. Christian life
  I. Title II. Porter, David, *1945–*
  248.4 BV4501.2

ISBN 0 551 01190 4

Typeset by Brian Robinson, North Marston, Bucks.

Printed in Great Britain by
Anchor Brendon Ltd, Tiptree, Essex.

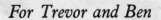

For Trevor and Ben

Contents

Preface

In 1977 I was arrested, tried and imprisoned in Bangkok on charges of smuggling heroin. While in prison, I became a Christian. After three years I was released by Royal amnesty and was allowed to return home.

I have told the story of my arrest and imprisonment in *Freed for Life*[1]. Many who have read that book have asked me about events since my release and about the work I now do with Prison Christian Fellowship, and that is why I have now taken the story further in this book. You don't need to have read *Freed for Life* before reading *Freed for Ever*; but as the story is a continuation, people and situations from the Far East and Bangkok women's prison appear in this book as well. For those who have not read *Freed for Life*, I have provided a short summary at the end of the book.

Since I returned to England, I have been helped and encouraged by many people from all walks of life. Here are just some of those I would like to thank.

First and foremost I would like to thank the many people who continue to uphold me in prayer. Without them I don't believe that this book, or the story that it contains, would have been possible.

From the early days of Prison Christian Fellowship, I would like to thank Ross Simpson, Sylvia-Mary Alison,

---

1. *Freed for Life*, by Rita Nightingale with David Porter (Marshalls, 1982).

Rev. John Harris, Tom Marriot and Tony Ralls; and more recently, Rev. Peter Timms, Peter Chadwick and Brian Stephenson. A special thank you to Christine Austen for her invaluable help in getting my programme and myself organised.

Rev. Herrick and Judy Daniels, Mona and Val Horsefield, Bob and Sheila Allison, Jim Hodson and Win ('Mother') Morgan all gave me friendship and spiritual help when I needed it most. I owe a debt of gratitude also to Chuck Colson, Kathryn Grant, Ferne Sanford, Gordon Loux, Jeanne Hurley, Peggy Morris and many more dear friends in the USA.

A big thank you to David and Tricia Porter for their hard work and late nights working on this book.

Thanks also to my wonderful family for love and understanding, through times which must have seemed so odd to them.

And last but not least, I would like to thank my dear Trevor, who married me in spite of all my shortcomings.

Rita Nightingale

Acknowledgements

In working with Rita on this, our second book, I have been given a great deal of help by various individuals and organisations.

Out of many who have contributed information and facts I would like to thank the following: the management of the Stirk House Hotel, Gisburn; Rev. Herrick Daniels; Mr. Ross Simpson; and Mr. and Mrs. Gilbert Kirby. Sylvia Mary Alison's *God is Building a House* (Marshalls, 1984) came to my notice very late in the project, but provides an interesting perspective on the growth of Prison Christian Fellowship in the UK. I am also grateful to Mrs. Barbara Rees for permission to use the quotation on page 179.

I have been given free access to Rita's notebooks, correspondence and other documentation. Information on matters American has been provided by Millie Thomson, Elaine Cooper and Liz Newman. Os House and staff have supplied crucial technical assistance in emergencies. The manuscript has been read in whole or in part by several people whose comments have been invaluable, including Pam Hendry and Jane Winter.

It remains to acknowledge the help and encouragement of Edward and Ann England, the wise counsels of my brother Peter Elsom, and the apparently limitless energy of my wife Tricia, who not only did an enormous amount of typing on this project but was also one of the manuscript's most discerning readers.

David Porter

1: England Again

Suddenly, unexpectedly, astonishingly, she was to be free. Five dizzying days and half-a-world later, her voice came softly, almost inaudibly . . . 'There are no words to describe the joy and the happiness.'

Jubilee (The newsletter of Prison Fellowship), March 1980

I was half-asleep, half-awake. My eyelids were screwed tight, trying to create some darkness. But the light was too strong. It was too strong every night. You couldn't bury your face in the pillow because after a while you had to shift to let some air at your face. The heat was static, a forest swelter, a moist tide lapping gently at legs and arms, creeping even into the towel wrapped round the head against insects and the naked light-bulb glaring monotonously down from the insect-crawling ceiling. *Oh, for a night with the light off!* But the light stayed on. That was the rule.

I lay rigid and motionless. I had learned to sleep that way. You had to. When you were sleeping with a regimented row of others, allocated three floorboards for yourself and your possessions, you learned quickly. Those who didn't were bullied into conformity by grunts, obscenities, and the occasional well-aimed kick or punch.

I shifted at last, and allowed my body to relax. It must be nearly six o'clock. Time to get up, to join the queue of others clutching their belongings in worn cardboard boxes, waiting for a turn at the dipper-bath to wash off the sweat of the night. Best catch a few extra moments' sleep. One more night got through. One more day ticked off the calendar. One day nearer 'going out', leaving Lard Yao Prison, leaving the crowded hot cells and the perpetual smell of stale fish and drying garbage. But it was never a good idea to start thinking about that day. Thinking about it could drive a girl mad.

'Rita! Rita – wake up!' Somebody was pulling at my shoulder. I grumbled complainingly, resentful at losing any precious moments of sleep. In some ludicrous corner of my memory I could smell breakfast, English breakfast. I shut the thought from my mind. But other scraps of England drifted into my half-awake thoughts. Then, as I struggled back to consciousness, from an ocean's depth of tiredness, I heard my mother's voice.

'Come on, love. Come on – you've been dreaming.'

I finally opened my eyes. The light that had been hurting them was a crisp January morning sun streaming through a neatly curtained window. Mum was holding me, rocking me gently awake. A tray of breakfast things lay on a table. Like shadows evaporating when a light shines brightly, Lard Yao and its inhabitants faded away. I was in bed, at home, in Blackburn, England. The nightmare was over.

It was a fortnight since I had arrived at London Airport on the last stage of my journey home from Bangkok. Three years in Lard Yao had burned many memories into my mind – some harrowing, some pleasant. I'd left good friends behind in prison, and other people to whom I'd been delighted to say goodbye. The same sights and sounds had dominated my life for so long; that hot courtyard, the vegetable beds bordering the prison sewer, the nursery

14

room with its perpetual stench of rag nappies, the lines of Thai prisoners chanting Bhuddist devotions as they shuffled forward into the prison refectory – each mental image at the time as sharp as a finely focused photograph and as irremovable as a tattoo.

And yet, two weeks after the exhilarating events of my release, those memories were patchy and fading; it was often impossible to remember what some of my fellow-prisoners even looked like, try as I might. My mind was beginning to be filled with homely details such as I had not witnessed for years. It was still all a bit of a jumble, a haze of emotion and excitement. Isolated moments stood out, little flashes of sharp detail in an unconnected chain of events.

That expensive carpet, for example, in a long, well-furnished corridor in a London hotel – I hadn't the slightest idea which hotel it was. After my arrival at the airport I had been driven there with Uncle George, by representatives of the *Daily Mail*, the national newspaper which had paid for my journey back to England. I'd been bubbling with excitement, and when I'd seen the plush carpet extending down the elegant corridor, I hadn't been able to resist temptation. To the astonishment of two hotel guests who happened to be in the corridor at the time, I'd turned a cartwheel on the spot. The feel of that carpet underfoot stuck in my mind as an almost tangible memory, its impossible softness cushioning the soles of my feet, still tanned and leathery from years of eastern roads and dusty prison yards.

My crazy cartwheel took me past the door to which our small party had been heading. We retraced our steps. Uncle George pushed the door open and stood back to let me go in. Sitting in the room waiting for me were my sister June and my mother.

The last time I'd seen Mum had been in Bangkok, over two years before, when I had been sullen and angry. I had

15

bitterly regretted many times the fact that she'd had to return home with only the memory of my rebellious, scared face watching her out of the prison office-block. Now, when I saw her again, I could only think how much older she looked, older even than she had seemed after the exhausting flight from England to Lard Yao. We clung to each other and wept – I think everybody in the room was crying. I said nothing to Mum, just repeated over and over again, 'Mum, Mum . . .' She said nothing to me. We just held each other for a long time. I was only conscious of the love that surrounded me that moment, and the fact that I was back with my family at last.

Time went by unnoticed. We must have been several hours in that room, hours which were now just a blur of happiness. I was too joyful to take in much. There was champagne, and the Press were there, and a great deal of talking was going on. I just sat on the floor, Thai-fashion (for weeks I would find it impossible to sit comfortably in a chair again), and every now and then I would reach out a hand and touch my Mum, to reassure myself that we were together again, that the long nightmare was really over.

When things had calmed down a little, Mum said, 'What do you want to do, Rita? Would you like to stay here for the night? You can, you know.'

I shook my head. 'I want to go home.'

We left the hotel in two cars. Uncle George and June went in one and I went in the other with Mum. There were journalists and photographers with us. I took in little of the journey north; it was dark anyway. I just held on to her. Once I turned to her and gave her an enormous bear-hug. She smiled gently.

'Go easy,' she chided, 'that's my sore shoulder.'

'What've you been doing?'

'I don't know – strained it, or something. It's taking its time to get better. Sign of old age.'

'Get away with you, Mum!' I laughed. She nodded at the

roadsigns flashing past the car as it raced on.

'We're not going straight home,' she said. 'You wouldn't get any peace. I haven't been there for a week. There are reporters banging at the door all day long. Ever since we heard you were coming home. We changed the phone number. You've no idea.'

I grinned at her happily. She might have been reading the Bangkok telephone directory aloud, for all I heard of what she said.

During the long journey we stopped at a motorway service station. The harshly lit dining area seemed like a scrubbed, gleaming palace. I hesitated for what seemed an age choosing between tea and coffee. It was the luxury of choice that made me linger. In the end the others chose for me. I sat absorbed in the newness of it all, playing with a paper sachet of sugar. How long since I last saw one of those?

My mother was wearing a lovely coat with a silver-fox fur collar, and as we sat at the table she took it off and put it round my shoulders. I must have looked an odd sight. I was wearing new clothes which had been sent out to Bangkok when I was released, and I probably looked quite smart. But on my feet I wore my comfortable Thai sandals that I had worn in prison. It had been so long since I had worn shoes that I couldn't go back to wearing them immediately.

'Let me try your shoes, Mum,' I said suddenly. She took them off and I slid my feet into them and stood up. The high heels felt as if someone had put bricks under my feet. It was like learning to walk in grown-up shoes all over again. I tottered a few paces and gave up. 'I'll have to work on it,' I laughed. I stared happily at the other people in the service station and put my sandals back on. After a while I kicked them off again and put them in my bag.

Back in the car I cuddled up to Mum.

The night rolled back before us as we sped north.

Suddenly, we were driving through Blackburn town centre. I stared through the windscreen, pointing out landmarks I hadn't seen for several years.

'Hey, Mum! Look at that! That's where what's-her-name used to live . . . Wow, we didn't have a Debenham's store when I left . . . Oh, look, that's changed . . . And your friend Florrie lived down that street . . .'

'You know this place better than I do,' said Mum good-humouredly.

'I want to see Ann,' I said. 'When will I see Ann?'

'She'll be there when we arrive.' Mum was solid, reassuring. It was all going to be all right.

We emerged the other side of Blackburn and finally pulled to a stop in front of an old-fashioned mansion. We must have driven almost to the Yorkshire border. We got out of the cars. I pulled Mum's coat more tightly round me. I was so dazed and light-headed that I couldn't understand what the building was.

'Is this Ann's house?'

Mum shook her head and indicated a hotel sign discreetly placed at the door. 'It's called the Stirk House Hotel.'

We went in. It was not far off midnight, a cold January night. I was wearing Mum's fur coat; my feet were bare. I must have looked weird, but I didn't care about the stares and whispers. The first person I saw was my Auntie Mary, changed since I had last seen her – her arthritis was no better, and she had put on some weight in the face – but instantly recognisable; and standing behind her, looking really beautiful, was my sister Ann. The lounge was full of people, but I had no eyes for anybody else. I went up to my Auntie Mary, kneeled down, and rested my head on her knee. Once again, I felt wrapped round by the wholeness and the love which I had not known for so long.

At the mealtable there were about twenty of us. Many of the faces I didn't know. Most were people who had been involved with my family in the campaign for my freedom.

Some had been helping Mum out by answering the phone for her or dealing with the press. Others were from the *Daily Mail*, and had been organising the details of my journey home and the arrangements at the hotels. Ian Smith of the *Mail*, who had flown to Bangkok to meet me and had escorted me back to London, was there; and so was his photographer, whom I had already met. I was introduced to lots of people and forgot their names as soon as I'd been told them. It was a cheerful, boisterous meal, and I was hardly conscious of any of it.

The other guests in the hotel were unaware of the reason for the celebrations. Auntie Mary told me later that the maitre d'hotel had stood at the door all evening, consulting his watch and frowning. Last orders for dinner had been taken at ten o'clock. As ten o'clock came and went, he had become increasingly agitated and had warned my aunt several times:

'If your party doesn't arrive soon it won't be possible to admit them.'

But during the meal he took Ann aside and confided to her, 'Now I understand who it is – it's fine, don't worry, everything is all right.'

Though it was so late when our meal was served, I enjoyed it enormously. I ordered steak, though I didn't eat much of it. I was too excited. I kept getting up from my seat and wandering round the other places, begging morsels of different food items to sample.

Afterwards we all went through to the lounge, a comfortable Lancashire lounge with polished horse-brasses on the oak-beamed fireplace, big armchairs and a little bar in one corner. Everybody was still talking, and I tried to be sociable. But I couldn't sit still for longer than two minutes at a time. I kept getting up and wandering round the room, picking up ashtrays and emptying them into the waste-paper basket. If I adjusted the curtains once I must have done so scores of times. I couldn't sit down for long and I couldn't find anything to hold my attention. I felt desperately tired, emotionally strung out and very, very happy.

The long day came to an end. I managed to get some sleep, but for much of the night I lay awake, my mind racing in a hundred different directions. What fitful dreams I had, merged into the general blur of the day's events.

2: At Stirk House

*Stirk House is a privately owned 16th
century manor house updated to a luxury
hotel . . . offering 'away from it all' seclusion
giving an immediate sense of relaxation . . .*

Hotel brochure

I woke up late the next day, somewhat stiff from the
unaccustomed luxury of a bed. It seemed as if I'd been
awake, on and off, most of the night, though I must have
slept for part of the time. I don't think an earthquake would
have stopped my body from insisting on *some* of the rest for
which it had been clamouring.

After the first disorientation everything came back into
sharp focus – the airport, meeting Mum, the long car
journey through the night, the joyful, disorganised time
together the previous evening. I looked around me
appreciatively. The bedroom at Stirk House was very nice,
and I was beginning to find beds bearable again – after my
release, on my way home from Bangkok I had stopped over
in Kuala Lumpur, and had had to sleep on the floor because
I wasn't used to anything else after prison.

I came downstairs into the forlorn, unoccupied
atmosphere that hotels have in the morning. From the
dining room came the sound of a vacuum cleaner whirring

away industriously, and I could see somebody laying the tables for lunch. Our celebrations of the previous night were a distant memory. I made my way to the lounge. Standing in the doorway, rubbing the sleep from my eyes, I gazed in disbelief at what I saw.

It seemed as though my whole family had packed into the room. All my aunts and uncles were there, and one by one they came and hugged me. They murmured lovely greetings – 'It's great to have you home', 'We're just so glad you're safe, Rita', 'Welcome back, love' – it was wonderful to see them. I'd heard bits of news of them all in letters that came to me in Bangkok, and you can piece together quite a good picture of how people are getting on from quite slender fragments of information. But we've always been a close family, and it had really hurt for three years knowing that I was locked away from any chance of coming home to them. I'd shed many tears at Christmas time, imagining them all enjoying the festivities at home. Now I was able to hold them, and kiss them, and tell them how much I had missed each one of them.

Ann hadn't stayed at the hotel overnight – she had gone home where John, her husband, was babysitting. Later that day she returned with the children, small strangers grown out of all recognition from the toddlers I had last seen; I wasn't sure whether they recognised me. Kathryn, now nine, stared at me curiously – I think she half-remembered who I was. Jonathan had been two when I left home and clearly had no idea who I might be. Emma, an eighteen-month old toddler, was the newly-conceived baby about whom Ann had told me when she visited me in Bangkok – I was the first to know she was pregnant. Now I was able to play with her baby.

The older children were quite unawed either by the occasion or the hotel and its grounds. My family stayed with me all day, and during a quiet lull I was relaxing cross-legged on the floor when Jonathan clambered onto my knee and delivered his verdict:

'Oh, Auntie Rita! I do like your house! I've just been in the swimming pool – it's great!'

It was a day for sandwiches and being together and walking in the countryside round the hotel. It was sheer delight to walk in the clean January sunlight, leaves crunching underfoot, hanging on to Ann with one arm and Mum with the other. I borrowed a fur coat from one of my aunts, and fur-lined boots from another. We chattered endlessly, about anything and everything. Bangkok seemed a million miles away. Over there it would be the hot season, but here everything was crisp winter green. It was as if I had been reborn into a new world of gusty skies and frosted hills. There were so many things that I had not seen for so long; the trees' bare outlines waiting for the new growth of spring, *stone* buildings, occasional walkers muffled and wrapped against the cold.

Back in the hotel, it was time for Ann and the children to go back home.

'Oh, by the way, Rita,' said Ann, 'this is yours.' She pointed to a large red sack in a corner of the lounge.

'Whatever is it?'

'It's your letters. We called at the house on our way here. They've been piling up for the last few days. They almost jammed the front door shut. The Post Office had so many the other day they sent them in the sack. Like a film star! Have a good time reading them.'

I pulled a corner of the sack open. Inside were what seemed like hundreds of envelopes, some tied in bundles.

'Wow! It's like my birthday all over again,' I grinned happily.

'Don't forget all the thank-you letters you'll have to write,' said Ann, and went to round up her children. Jonathan was reluctant to leave the fairytale palace.

'I'm hungry, Mummy,' he protested.

'Never mind, I'll get something to eat when we get home.'

'Don't do that, Mummy,' Jonathan reassured her. 'Just tell the servants to bring some more sandwiches, then we can eat now . . .'

Poor Jonathan! The staff of Stirk House had been serving afternoon tea for the past few hours, and he had watched wide-eyed as trays of cakes, sandwiches and pots of tea had appeared in seemingly limitless supply. Watching his face fall, I felt quite guilty. He must have thought that his Auntie Rita coming home meant the start of a quite different lifestyle!

Later I sat in the lounge enjoying the glowing fire, as warm as toast. June, Mum and two of my aunts were with me; I was sitting on the floor, leaning against Mum's chair. I was more comfortable that way. The sack of mail was open in front of me. I was pulling out letters and cards at random and reading them, sometimes aloud to my aunts. They were from people I didn't know, who had followed the story of my arrest and imprisonment and were now writing to welcome me home. They contained lovely messages, full of affection and kindness, some from Christians who had been praying for me, others from people who had contributed from their old-age pensions to help me while I was in prison.

'Look at this one,' I said, fishing out an orange envelope with official stamps all over it. 'It's a telegram!'

I tore it open and extracted the form inside.

'Who from?' asked Auntie Mary.

'It's from Chuck Colson in America. You know, he wrote that book I told you about. He works with prisoners in the States.' I scanned the telegram. 'He used to work for President Nixon. He was in the Watergate thing,' I added as an afterthought.

'What does he want?' said Mum.

'He wants me to telephone him reversed charges. In America. I wonder why?'

'Don't you go off on your travels again this week,' smiled Mum comfortably.

I looked at the telegram again. *Call collect*, it said, and gave the number – one of those long American telephone numbers.

We read more messages and admired the cards. We had barely got half-way through the sack when I stood up and stretched.

'I think I'll give my legs a bit of exercise,' I said. I bent down and picked the telegram up from where it lay in its bright envelope. I smoothed it out against the back of Mum's chair. Standing behind her, I stroked her head. How grey her hair was! Had it been like that before I went away?

'Do you know, Mum, I think I'll go and give Mr. Colson that phone call,' I said. She frowned.

'Now?' There was something indefinable in her voice. It sounded like fear.

'He was awfully kind to me, Mum. He sent Kathryn Grant to see me in Bangkok. That was how I found out about him. He runs Prison Fellowship over in the States.'

Mum grunted. 'Don't be long, love.'

I went upstairs to my bedroom and closed the door. I picked up the bedside telephone and asked the operator for a reversed charges connection to the number on the telegram.

It was early morning in America. Chuck Colson wasn't available, but I spoke to several of his colleagues. They were delighted to hear me; for several minutes I was greeted by one American voice after another, and there was a good deal of emotion at both ends of the telephone cable. Kathryn Grant had visited me in November when I had seventeen years of my sentence left and no prospect of release. Now I was home again, a mere four months later.

'It's the Presidential Prayer Breakfast next month,' they told me. 'Can you come over?'

'Come over?' I hadn't thought of moving outside Lancashire for the next few months, let alone England. In any case, I hadn't the slightest idea what might be so special about the President's breakfast.

'Rita, we would just love you to come to America and spend some time with us, there are so many people we want you to meet. And we want you to talk with some of our groups . . .'

'No!' I protested, laughing. 'I'm just home, you know? I'm not going anywhere, I want to be with my family!'

They were very understanding and we talked for what seemed a long time. They suggested a number of meetings and special events that they would like me to go over for, but I said no to all of them.

'Well, Rita, we understand that you need to take time to adjust. But please, do keep in touch. We'll write you. We believe that the Lord would have us share with you what we're doing. We'll keep in touch, Rita.'

For a while after replacing the receiver I continued to sit on my bed, deep in thought. It was wonderful to have felt such love and enthusiasm in the voices of those to whom I had been speaking. It was also just a little bit unsettling. Nothing could have been farther from my mind at that moment than travelling again. Oddly, it was the invitation, not the prospect of travel, that I found unnerving. I had no desire to travel again. It was a strange experience to be asked, however. It reminded me that eventually I would have to decide what I was going to do with the rest of my life. *Lord*, I said aloud, *please help me; all this is too much to handle.*

I stood up, tossed my head back, and went downstairs. Mum and my aunts were as I had left them. Mum looked up as I came into the lounge.

'How did it go?'

'Oh – fine,' I said off-handedly. I paused. 'They want me to go to America.'

My mother winced.

'I told them no,' I added hurriedly. 'I said I wanted to stay here with you.'

Mum visibly relaxed. 'Tell me about this Chuck Colson.'

I had told her a bit about him in letters, but this was different. I told her how he had been President Nixon's Special Counsel, one of his five top advisers, and had been sent to prison for his involvement in the Watergate conspiracy. He had become a Christian in the early days of the court proceedings, and after his release from prison he had had a vision of what God wanted for his life; to work among prisoners, showing them how much God loved them, building fellowships of Christians in every prison in America. That was the vision of Prison Fellowship, and that was the story that Kathryn Grant had told me when she visited me in Lard Yao in November 1979. She had brought me a copy of Chuck's new book, *Life Sentence*, which tells the story of how God brought the Fellowship into being and had made it grow.

I had read the book, fascinated. Everything that Kathryn had said struck a chord in my heart. I had been praying for some time for prisoners, not just those whom I knew in Lard Yao, but all the thousands I didn't know in prisons all over the world. Kathryn's visit showed me that God *did* care, that he had already inspired people to help those for whom I had such a burning concern.

Some of this I tried to share with Mum and the others. Of course, it led on to my own story, of how I had become a Christian in prison. It was a good time to chat; one of those relaxed, rambling sorts of conversations that you get into when you're feeling very happy and tired. I'd always been close to my aunts, and of course I wanted to share everything with Mum, so it was easy to talk to them about how I had come to believe in Jesus and what he had meant to me in prison.

I talked about my first bitterness and resentment, how I had stormed at Lucille and Margaret who had visited me faithfully for so long and talked to me about Jesus as if he might actually be a real person; and I told them about the day an elderly lady called Martha Livesey, travelling through Bangkok, had called at the prison to see me and announced that she too came from Blackburn. I had broken down in tears and fled to the darkest, most secret place I could find, and there, sitting sobbing under the prison hospital hut, I had read the tract she had left me and there I had given my life to God.

I was so happy to be able to talk freely to the people I loved the most, about the things that were now most important to me. They listened to all that I said. They knew a little of it already; from letters I knew that since her visit to Bangkok, Martha Livesey had gone to see Mum and had kept in contact with her since; now I was able to tell them myself what her visit had meant to me.

I wondered afterwards what had been going through their minds as I'd talked. I'd left home a dissatisfied, restless twenty-one year old; I'd gone from a wrecked marriage to a night club in Hong Kong and from there I had burst onto the front pages of the world's newspapers accused of smuggling drugs. Now I was back, radiantly happy, talking about my new-found faith as a Christian. Did it cross their minds, as it had crossed the minds of so many, that it might just be escapism – mere wishful thinking, a prisoner's comfort? Some had already 'explained' my conversion to me rationally: 'Well, you were distressed, of course you were. And you were on your own. That made it worse. And you were cut off from everything and everybody you knew. So you turned to religion. It gave you what you needed – peace of mind, something to live for. Oh, it's not your fault . . . lots of people do the same in that situation.'

That was what Hannah, my fellow-prisoner in Lard Yao, had said to me. To her and to others before and after my release I could only reply, 'It's not just peace of mind I needed. It wasn't a psychological thing at all. I met a *person*. I met Jesus. He changed my life.'

28

Suddenly, as I lay stretched out on my bed, thoughts of the future swept over me. I felt myself panicking. What would I do? How would I earn my living? What was going to happen? *I can't cope, Lord!*, I cried out in my heart. *I'm so confused . . .*

I was terrified. It all seemed so difficult.

Then I realised what I had instinctively done. *I've just cried out to God*, I thought, *and he was there where I looked for him*.

Since arriving at the airport I had barely prayed or read my Bible. But that didn't mean that I had forgotten God. Quite the opposite; in the midst of all the excitement and emotion I felt myself buoyed up by a great tide of his love, secure and protected, like sailing down a rushing river in a boat you trust perfectly. In all the things that were happening I lived each moment as it came, and all the time I knew the Lord was with me.

That night as I drifted off to sleep I drowsily reminded myself of how God had cared for me in the past week. On the plane, leaving Bangkok airport, I'd been overwhelmed by an enormous conflict inside me as the joy of freedom struggled with fear of the future. In Kuala Lumpur I'd been unable to sit at table without breaking down in floods of tears. My family in England must have been wondering in what sort of state they'd find me when I came home; yet I'd sat last night at dinner with all those people, and I'd been able to order a meal and hold some sort of a conversation, just a day or two after Kuala Lumpur. It was God's perfect planning, I knew. It had been my own spontaneous decision to come home via a roundabout way, nobody had advised me to; but by doing so I had gained some control of myself by the time I met Mum and my family.

I was very aware, in that hotel bedroom, of the presence of Jesus. I began to talk to him. I told him all the things that had happened that day, and how mixed up I was. I told him about meeting my family again, about being among people who loved me; and I told him about the phone call to America and the overflowing sack of mail. One by one I handed my joys and my worries to him. I felt a deep calm spreading inside me. Whatever the future might hold, it was in his hands. It really was going to be all right.

3: Blackburn

No-one who has not been locked away with the prospect of being caged for 20 years can appreciate the feeling of complete and utter freedom and happiness.

Interview with David Allin printed in the *Lancashire Evening Post*, 24 January 1980.

And then, next day, it all started to go wrong. It seemed unbelievable that anything could spoil the happiness and joy which had carried me along for two days. Maybe the strain of all the excitement was becoming too much for me. Maybe there were suddenly just too many people to cope with. Whatever the reason, on the third day back in England I snapped.

It started out a bad day. In the morning I continued to explore my sack of mail, and once again found numerous messages of goodwill and friendship. When I ripped open the insignificant white envelope with its scrawled name and address it seemed no different to any of the others.

Minutes later I was still staring at it in dumb horror. It was a typed letter, full of mistakes and mis-spellings, like one of those ransom notes you read about. The writer sounded as if he was eaten up with anger and vicious hatred.

You're back home now, I read. *You're in all the newspapers. But I know what you're really like. Soon the whole world will know. You'll be back the way you used to be . . .*

I gripped the letter in both hands and shakily tore it in two. Then I put the pieces together and tore them in two again. I threw the pieces on the floor, separate from the other letters. My hands were trembling. Nearby Mum and June were talking. A dull throbbing sounded in my ears. It was my pulse. I thought I was going to faint.

'Mum . . . oh Mum . . .'

She came across to find me clenching and unclenching my fists, fighting back huge sobs. When I looked at her I collapsed into floods of tears and pointed mutely at the pieces of the letter. I threw my arms round her and wept as she fitted them together and read the words grim-faced. Then she gripped my shoulders and pushed me back.

'Now look, woman,' she said fiercely. 'Just stop that at once.'

I stared at her wetly as she gathered up handfuls of the other letters and cards.

'Just *look* at what you've got,' she demanded. 'All these people, all glad to see you home, all full of kind things to say. You got all these, and when *one* person, one sick stupid *person*, writes a stupid letter – you go to pieces.'

She flung the letters up in the air and they fluttered down again like a flock of paper birds. The effort hurt her shoulder, and she sat back holding it as she watched for my reaction. 'All these good letters,' she repeated. After a few moments I nodded miserably and wiped a sleeve across my eyes. My sobs shuddered to a stop. Mum beamed.

'That's better, love. They're not worth it, people who would write a letter like that. They're sick, they're beneath contempt.'

She's right, I thought. *What does it matter? It matters nothing.* I went on reading the letters and cards, and by the time I got to the end of them without finding any more antagonistic letters; I was nearly back to normal, with only an occasional sniff betraying the fact that I was still upset.

The episode cast a shadow over the morning, and I was subdued with other people. My nerves were jangling, and I had a hot, thundering headache. Sooner or later it was inevitable that I would explode at somebody or other, and sure enough it happened.

What made it worse was that the person who took the brunt of it was somebody who had been extraordinarily kind to me – Ian Smith, the *Daily Mail* reporter whose paper had arranged for my flight back and the hotel and everything. It was part of a contract that the *Mail* made with my family at the time of my release, by which they were now entitled to exclusive rights on my story for a period. The contract stipulated that nothing was to be printed without my family's approval. Ian had never acted like somebody who had a commercial interest in my experiences. On the flight from Thailand, via Kuala Lumpur, he had been a relaxed, tolerant companion for somebody who was almost hysterical with delight and emotionally totally erratic. In so many ways, I doubt if there could have been a better escort.

On the plane back from Kuala Lumpur, I had poured out almost my entire life story to him. He hadn't pressed me to say anything; in fact he went out of his way to say that if I wanted to sleep all the way home, that was fine. But once I'd started talking it was impossible to stop.

During that morning Ian walked into the lounge and handed me a copy of that day's *Daily Mail*.

'Well, there you are, Rita. What do you think of it?'

I took the paper from him hesitantly. There, on the front page, was a picture of me, laughing and crying at the same time, and a paragraph saying that this was Rita Nightingale who'd been released from prison and that the full story was on the centre pages. I blinked at the picture. It was disconcerting because I hadn't realised what a sight I had looked – it was taken before the Consular officials had allowed me the use of what had seemed to be the most wonderful bathroom in the world. I smiled cautiously at Ian and turned to the centre pages. My mouth fell open in shock.

It was the first time that I'd seen any major coverage of my story in the press. Friends and relatives had sent me various cuttings in Lard Yao, and when I was released I'd been shown a newspaper photo of Mum back home in Blackburn just after she'd been told the news. But it was a different experience to open up a whole newspaper and find that the centre spread was about me.

In fact Ian had hardly used anything of what I told him on the plane. He'd been very sensitive and hadn't exploited the fact that I was telling everything regardless. He'd taken a number of small parts of the story and put them together, and had checked the whole thing with Ann and obtained her permission. Ann, of course, had been getting letters from me all the time, as had the rest of my family, so she was able to make sure that the story was told in an accurate way as far as was possible. In fact, when you realise that he had been as well placed as anybody could be to exploit and sensationalise my story, his handling of the whole thing was miraculously gentle and considerate.

But that morning, I didn't think of that at all. I just stared numbly at the article. There was Maria's story, poor sick Spanish Maria who had been old enough to be my mother. She had come to Lard Yao, charged with being the accomplice of a drugs dealer; she spoke no English. Despite that, we had become very close, and when I became a Christian we began to read the Bible together, I with my English Bible, she with a Spanish one that had been sent to her by Christians in England. We used to show each other verses we'd found and look them up, each in our respective languages. In due course she went to court, and was sentenced to forty years. The news shattered her; shortly afterwards she had a nervous breakdown. Just before I left lard Yao, I had visited her in her dark, foul-smelling cell, where she had sat with her back to me, staring blankly at the wall, ignoring my voice. *Oh, Maria, love! How could I bear it, to leave Bangkok without saying goodbye?* But it had been no use. My last sight of her had been of her soiled, bent shoulders.

And now Maria's story was all over the centre pages of the *Daily Mail*, for anybody to read. Details of our friendship which I'd mentioned in letters home were reprinted in bold type. I stared at the page in blank misery. A jumble of bitter thoughts ran one after the other through my mind. Here was I, free and with my family; Maria was still in her cell, dirty and afraid. I felt dirty too. It was like a betrayal; not just that I had betrayed Maria but that Ian had betrayed me.

I rounded on him, waving the paper in his face. 'How can you do a thing like that to me?'

My voice sounded high-pitched and wobbly. I didn't care.

Ian looked taken aback. 'I'm not sure that . . .'

'You're horrible! How *could* you? You put it in a *newspaper*, about *Maria*. I hate you, I *hate* you!'

I could see I'd hurt him, but I didn't try to soften the force of what I'd said. I turned on my heel and flounced out of the room. Mum tried to stop me – I just pushed past. One or two hotel guests who'd watched the whole thing looked curious or embarrassed.

I stormed to the nearest telephone and dialled Ann's number. Her quiet voice answered.

'Rita, what's wrong?'

I blurted out my anger.

'It's horrible, it's awful, you've got to come over to the hotel. Oh Ann, it's *horrible* . . .'

I had lost control of myself. It was a real tantrum. Part of me was watching how I was behaving with a fascinated detachment, quite unable to stop it. By the time Ann and John arrived I was trembling and incoherent. John took one look at me, at my streaked and woebegone features.

'Come on,' he said. He put his arm protectively round my shoulders. 'Wash your face, I'm taking you out.'

We got into the car and he drove me into Gisburn village. By the time we got there I was already beginning to calm down. John parked the car near the old Norman church, and we went in to look around.

Multi-coloured sunlight dappled through the stained glass windows, and the noises of the village traffic were subdued as I wandered around the lovely old church. I walked to the front and stood before the altar with its great window behind, and almost without thinking I knelt.

As I knelt there I realised what the trouble was. For the past few days I'd been so conscious of God's love and care, and then in the shock of seeing the hateful letter and the newspaper I'd forgotten he was there at all. Now I just wanted to talk to him again. *Lord,* I said silently, *I don't know what's happening to me. But I know you're with me. You've got to help me to cope, because I don't understand any of this.*

John waited patiently for me at the back of the church, and after a while we left and went into the local gift shop. I felt much better, and the turmoil inside me was already subsiding. I began to enjoy myself again.

I couldn't believe all the beautiful things in that shop. I picked up one thing after another — frivolous chiffon scarves, suede-leather gifts, lots of things — and gazed at them entranced, touching and stroking them. At my side, John bought a few things, and the other people in the shop were looking at us with great interest. I was so obviously excited, he was buying things, and every now and then I hugged him for sheer happiness. After a while one of them said to John, 'Is it your anniversary?'

I giggled, and John smiled and replied mysteriously, 'No, it's not our anniversary. But it's a very special day.'

Then I felt a kindly hand on my shoulder. It was the lady who ran the shop.

'I know who you are.' She had a comfortable, reassuring voice. 'You know, we always believed you were innocent. And we're so happy you've come home.'

When we left the shop we didn't say anything as we started back to the car. Then John broke the silence. 'I reckon that's what most people think,' he remarked quietly.

It was the first time that I had talked with any of my family about the court proceedings, and it was the first time since coming home that I had had any contact with people who were not directly concerned with my case. Those few words from the lady in the shop meant more to me than I can say.

We went back to the hotel. I found Ian Smith and apologised.

'I'm really sorry. I think it's probably seeing it the first time in print.' I fumbled for the right words. 'It's not that you wrote anything bad, really it's not, it's just that for me it's still . . . still memories, you know?'

He was very kind, and said I wasn't to worry. But I felt I'd hurt him, and I felt bad about it. He could have written so much more, but he didn't. His paper had paid for the travel and the hotels – our family could never have afforded anything like it. He got the exclusive story, but I am still grateful to him for his restraint in telling it.

'I want to go home, Mum.'

It was later the same day, and I'd recovered from the upsets earlier. But now as I looked around the comfortable hotel and the countryside outside, I found myself thinking longingly of Blackburn.

We packed, and Ian Smith drove me and Mum back to Mum's house. I'd never been there, because it was a council house to which she had moved since I'd left home. I had a rough idea where it was, because she'd told me all about it in letters, but as we drove through the gathering early dusk I began to be very excited. It was dark by the time we got there, and we had to go through a complicated performance to which by now my family was well used – Ian stopped the car a little way from the house, and somebody went to see whether there were any reporters waiting at the front door. There were, and we ended up going round behind the house and creeping in secretly through the back door to escape them.

I didn't pay much attention to all that. I was so excited, I was skipping up and down, and when we were in the house I explored every nook and cranny.

'Oh, Mum, it's lovely!'

It really was. All our old treasures and knick-knacks were there, and since she'd moved house she'd bought new furniture and curtains.

At the door Ian Smith said he ought to be getting back, and after we had said our goodbyes and expressed our gratitude he left. We bolted the doors. We were alone together at last.

The house had been empty for several days, and though Mum turned the heat on it took a while for the room to warm up. June began to tidy things and put some tea things on the table. I still felt cold, and kept my coat on as I sat on the floor. *How small it is in here*, I thought; but looking round I realised that it wasn't that the room was particularly tiny. It was just that it was closed in – the door was shut, the curtains drawn. That might seem an odd reaction when you think that I had just spent three years in prison, but the cells in Lard Yao had been large dormitories, with open windows.

But it wasn't long before I got used to it, and I was much more interested in the gleaming bathroom upstairs. Soon I was revelling in the luxury of a hot bath. I'd soaked in several such since my release, and the novelty hadn't worn thin yet. For three years I'd washed by pouring water over myself from a tin dipper filled from a dripping tap, with a string of prisoners behind me grumbling for their turn. Now it seemed as though I had all the time and all the hot water in the world. I sighed blissfully, relaxed, and enjoyed myself.

4: Starting Again

*For Rita it was her prayers, and the prayers
of others who believed in her, that opened the
gates of Lard Yao.*

*And as she said farewell to Thailand, she
declared: 'I intend to devote the rest of my
life to repaying that trust.'*

Daily Express 25 January 1980

'Are you all right, love?' asked Mum curiously. I jerked
myself awake, blinked and smiled vaguely.

'Oh, I'm fine, Mum – just tired, that's all.' I uncurled
myself from the corner of the room where I'd been
snatching a few minutes rest. It was late afternoon, I'd been
home two days, and the family had thrown a party to
celebrate my return. It had been a non-stop party ever since
I'd got home – my aunts and uncles popped in every few
hours, it seemed, to take another look at their long-lost
niece; and neighbours called round to say 'Hello' and
'Welcome home'. Of course everybody who came was
invited indoors for a cup of tea, and Mum's living room had
seemed like Manchester Central Station at times.

It was all lots of fun, and it was lovely to see old friends
and neighbours, some of whom had written to me in prison,
and some whose news had been passed on to me in letters

from Mum. But at bedtime, when we locked the door and sat together on our own, Mum, June and I would look at each other with relief. The non-stop celebration was becoming an emotional and physical strain for my family as well as for me, and during those first few days living back with my family I was beginning to realise how bad the past years had been for them.

Watching Mum sipping her tea that afternoon, massaging her stiff shoulder and wincing with tiredness, I hoped that the excitement would die down soon.

'I'm just a *bit* tired,' I repeated, and made my way across the room to where Uncle George and Aunt Mary were in animated conversation. Mum followed me across. Uncle George beamed at me.

'Well – how's the lady in the news?'

I grimaced, and laughed. He frowned suddenly. 'You know,' he said, 'you do look washed out. Are you getting enough sleep?'

Mum agreed vigorously. 'That's what I've been saying to her, George. Look at her. Matchsticks couldn't keep those eyes open much longer.'

Uncle George peered into my eyes in mock scrutiny and nodded sagely. 'Best thing for you is bed, Rita. No, really, you ought to let us all get on with it. You disappear upstairs. You shouldn't be trying to socialise. You're wiped out.'

'Ah, come on, Uncle George!' I protested. 'I told you – I can hardly sleep at night, let alone in the afternoon. I've got to get used to sleeping properly again. I can't make it happen.'

Mum interrupted. 'That's what you say, lovey. I'm packing you off to bed. Now.'

'Best place for her,' said Uncle George.

Auntie Mary put her arm round me. 'You take it easy, love. Plenty of time for staying up late when you've got used to being home.'

'But it's only five o'clock . . .!' I grumbled, but as Mum took my arm and led me out I was quite glad to have had the matter taken out of my hands. *Come to think of it,* I decided, *I really am zonked. Maybe I will be able to sleep.*

'Auntie Rita! Auntie Rita!'

Somebody a thousand miles away was calling my name. I recognised the voices of Ann's children. So Ann had arrived. It would be nice to go down and see her. I lay in the darkened room with my eyes closed, wondering what time it was. There were still people downstairs, I could hear voices. As I was trying to decide whether to get up or not, I dozed again. I was half-aware of the children rattling the doorknob and calling my name again, and of somebody taking them away. After a while I half-woke. It was a lot quieter downstairs. Most of the visitors must have gone. I stretched and moved restlessly. The bedroom door eased open a fraction. Mum came in and drew the curtains closer together. I smiled at her drowsily and she kissed my forehead.

Before long I fell into a deep sleep, and knew nothing more until I woke up late the next morning. I had slept for over fifteen hours. 'Did I really sleep properly, Mum?' I demanded. She smiled reassuringly. 'Like a log, Rita. I popped in every now and then all through the evening, and you were fast asleep.'

Many difficulties were sorted out by that long sleep. I hadn't realised just how tired I had been. For over a week I had been surviving on nervous energy, robbing my body of rest and making up for it by sheer excitement. The practical difficulty of adjusting to sleeping in a bed again had made matters worse. I realised now that my tiredness was part of the cause of my outburst at Ian Smith, and that it lay behind my inability to do anything other than drift with events and shut the future out of my mind.

But now my body was rested, and so was my mind. I began to pick up the threads of normal life again. I read through each of the letters in the red sack again, and that gave me something definite to do in my first few days at home. Sometimes I was moved to tears, often to prayer, as I read the messages of welcome and affection.

Among the letters was one from a lady called Sylvia Mary Alison. She was the wife of a Member of Parliament. She wrote to welcome me home, saying that she had been told about me in America by Chuck Colson. She told me a little about the Prison Christian Fellowship in England, which was a group linked with the American organisation. It had begun in 1979, and now had quite a large membership.

I was interested to read about the Fellowship, and excited to know that the Lord was moving people in England as he had in America. But I didn't answer her letter then; I didn't answer any of the letters. None seemed to expect an answer and I was incapable of sitting down in one place for ten minutes, let alone the several days it would have taken to reply to each one individually. My decision not to reply to the letters in no way meant that I didn't care or appreciate the fact that so many had written. I just wasn't capable of dealing with the situation beyond thanking the Lord for every person who had taken the time to write to me, which I did.

I began to set aside time to pray again, and to read my Bible. And over the next days and weeks, I began to adjust to being an unemployed Blackburn girl, after three years of being a notorious foreign prisoner in a Thai jail.

The national Press lost interest in my story quite quickly, and because Mum had agreed that the *Daily Mail* should have exclusive rights to the story, I didn't have to talk to other daily newspapers. Soon other stories dominated the front pages, for which I was profoundly glad.

Local interest continued for much longer. Some of it was embarrassing, some hurtful, but mostly it was warm and affectionate. I had a rough time being interviewed on Radio

Blackburn shortly after I came home – the interviewer was quite hostile. But I'd expected that, and had decided to do the interview anyway because it was a way of being able to thank publicly all the people who had worked and campaigned locally for my release. The *Lancashire Evening Telegraph* had staged a magnificent campaign of articles, but also local people had helped in scores of ways – I heard of pensioners who had put hard-earned coins in collecting boxes, and other people who had worked unpaid to help publicise my case. I didn't even know who some of them were – they had never met me, nor I them. Even if I had had time to thank each of them personally I would not have been able to find them all to do so. Going on the radio was one way I could say a general 'Thank you'.

Apart from that one radio programme I turned down every request for interviews. Some time after I came home I opened the front door one day to a man who turned out to be a reporter from one of the national Sunday newspapers.

'We would be very interested in running your story,' he said. I shook my head.

'I'm sorry, I don't want to.'

The reporter grinned at me. 'It's money in your pocket,' he said, and named a figure that seemed astronomical.

'I'm not interested,' I said flatly, and wondered at myself for refusing such a handsome offer. But I found the idea offensive. Reading Ian's article had upset me, and that had been a careful, sensitive handling of what I had been through. The thought of selling a story about all the people still in prison, so that I could have lots of money to enjoy my freedom while they were still inside, made me feel slightly sick.

The reporter looked surprised. I wondered if he thought I was trying to raise his price. The idea hadn't entered my head. 'It's not the money,' I explained. He nodded sympathetically.

'Of course we'd put in about your religious experiences.'

Some chance, in that newspaper, I thought, remembering other big stories they had run in the past.

'I thought . . .'

But I said no, and eventually he left, presumably to go back to London.

'You are thoughtless,' Mum chided me. 'You didn't even invite him in for a cup of tea.'

One day Ann took me with her to Chorley, the town near Blackburn where she lived. It was market day, and we wandered round the stalls. Nobody recognised me, and I enjoyed going unnoticed. It had been raining, and we tried to avoid the drips of water trickling off the edges of the stalls onto our necks. We laughed a lot as we crammed with others into the sheltered patches in front of the counters.

I loved hearing people's voices, being surrounded by shoppers all speaking English – and not only English, but proper, Lancashire English at that! And there was so much to see, and such a choice. I suppose that now I would think it a very ordinary market much like any other, but that day it was like Aladdin's cave. There was so much on offer, and such a wide choice of goods. In a poor country, like many in the Far East, the markets that the residents use are functional and you buy what you can find. In Chorley I browsed for a long time comparing several rival fruit stalls. It was the same when we went on to a large supermarket where Ann did her weekly shopping. Freedom of choice, I was beginning to realise, is a great luxury.

'Here,' said Ann, 'would you carry these?'

She handed me two plastic carrier bags full of purchases. I took them, and she reorganised her own load of shopping and children. I was shocked to find that I could hardly carry the bags. I'd done no strenuous exercise for so long, and this was the first time I'd attempted to lift anything heavy. Up to then I'd been cosseted like royalty, with reporters carrying my bags and everything done for me. As I gritted my teeth and dragged the bags along the supermarket floor – making sure Ann didn't see, because she was heavily loaded herself – I realised that I was going to have to get back into shape.

Then Ann did turn round and see me struggling. We both began to giggle hysterically, and bystanders watched in perplexity trying to work out what was so funny about two perfectly normal carrier bags.

It was some time before I could feel entirely comfortable out of doors in Blackburn. I went shopping with June in Blackburn market one day, and there people did recognise me. As I went from stall to stall I saw people glancing at me and then openly staring. I glared back at them at first but then began to try to hide myself, turning my back on bystanders and looking distractedly at the goods on display.

'I don't like it, June. I want to go home.'

I prayed about the problem and talked it over with Mum and June. We realised that I would either have to become a paranoid recluse or just get on with my life. I decided on the latter. I learned to ignore the stares and even respond to some of the friendlier looks with an answering smile. *After all*, I reasoned, *when you think about the publicity there's been about me in Blackburn it would be stupid to expect anything else.*

In any case, there were so many new things to be tried and enjoyed. I insisted on always going upstairs on the bus, and on sitting in the front seat so that I could see everything that there was to be seen. Even at home when everybody else was out I revelled in the solitude, and paced from room to room marvelling at the peaceful quietness of Mum's house. After three years in a crowded prison I had forgotten what it was like to hear faint sounds in the distance, like a car starting up or children shouting some blocks away. In Lard Yao, there were few faint sounds.

It was like being a little girl again, when everything

seemed to be new and most things appeared highly amusing.

Going to church was a very special new experience. I'd been before, of course, on various occasions before I left home, but this was different. Now I was a Christian, I was a member of God's family, and going to church and joining in with the worship was bound to be a totally new experience. I'd occasionally allowed myself to think about it in prison, on the rare occasions when I'd permitted myself to dream of the life I'd live when I was released.

Finding a church had seemed an impossible task. When I was released I had said my last farewells in Bangkok to Jack and Gladys Martin, the missionaries who had visited Lard Yao regularly for Bible classes and had watched over my first faltering steps as a Christian. 'I don't know any Christians there,' I told them. 'I don't know which church to go to or anything like that.'

'You'll be all right,' Jack had replied. 'The Lord has his hand on your life, we know that. He is going to protect you and use you.'

Jack's words were fulfilled sooner than either of us realised. During the first week of my return home, I had a telephone call.

'Hello,' said a pleasant voice. 'I'm Bob Allinson. I and my wife Sheila live in Blackburn. We read you were back, in the *Evening Telegraph*. Welcome home.'

I had had a number of calls like that from well-wishers. 'Thanks for ringing,' I said. 'I appreciate it very much. It's great being back.' I waited to hear if Mr. Allinson had anything else to say. He had.

'I don't want to intrude,' he said, 'and I know it'll be quite strange for you for a while getting things back to normal again. But the reason I rang is to say that if you and your mother would like to come to church with Sheila and me on Sunday, we'd love to see you. And would you be free to have lunch with us afterwards?'

'That's really kind of you,' I said. I hesitated. 'I'm afraid we haven't got a car – I don't know whether we could get to you.'

'No problem,' he replied easily. 'We can pick you up.'

So on Sunday all four of us went to the Methodist church near his home. When we went in I was quite apprehensive. It felt as though everybody was staring at me – I hadn't spent much time out of doors yet, and still felt very vulnerable. Probably they weren't looking at me, but I was sure they were and I was afraid that afterwards, they would want to buttonhole me and ask me all about Bangkok. *I just want to be me*, I thought. *I don't want to be somebody 'different'*.

Bob and Sheila were ideal hosts. They didn't announce who I was or introduce me to people with a great commotion. We just went in and sat down quietly.

I gazed around with a mounting sense of joy. After two years of being a Christian almost on my own in prison, I was meeting with a group of others in church for the first time. The most lovely part of it all was the singing. I'd never been able to sing heartily with a large congregation in Lard Yao because there wasn't one. More than that, I was singing with understanding. In school assembly and in Sunday School as a child, I'd enjoyed singing hymns and had raised my voice with great enthusiasm. But I hadn't had much of an idea at all of what the words meant. Now every word had meaning. I was so excited by some of the words that I jumped up and down as I sang.

I didn't take in much of the sermon. It was a long time since I'd listened to somebody talking at length about Christianity and been obliged to sit still and keep my questions and comments to myself! So I contented myself with sitting quietly and thinking about God and talking to him, silently, thanking him for allowing me to be in church.

Afterwards we stood for a while in the church grounds, enjoying the winter sunshine. One or two people recognised me because they'd seen my face in the papers, and they came up to say hello, but there wasn't any sense of pressure. I was pleased that most people didn't recognise me. I suppose it was an unrealistic hope, but I wanted to put all the notoriety of the past behind me, and just be a normal person again. That ideal saw me through the first few months of my return to England, and in the Methodist church that first Sunday I was able to imagine that I was almost unknown.

Afterwards we had lunch with Bob and Sheila at their home. We talked about the service.

'It was wonderful,' I said thoughtfully. 'But I really think we ought to look for a church nearer home. Not having a car makes such a difference. It would be nice to go to a local church anyway.'

'That's fair enough,' said Bob. 'What d'you think, Sheila? St. Andrews is a good evangelical church. It might be the answer.'

Sheila nodded. 'Yes, I think you'd like it,' she smiled. Mum looked up.

'Is that the one just down the road from us? I used to know the Vicar there. Not the one that's there now, the one before him. He was a really nice man.'

We decided that next Sunday we would go to St. Andrews.

Next week Mum had a telephone call while I was out shopping.

'Mrs. Livesey rang,' she told me.

I was thrilled. I'd been longing to see her again, and had planned to visit her as soon as I could. She was living in Blackpool now.

'*Martha*! How is she? What did she say? Did she give you a message for me?'

'Slow down, love! She's coming to see you.'

'Wow! That's amazing! When?'

'She's visiting her sister here in Blackburn, and she'll call and see us.'

A few days later I was upstairs when the doorbell rang. I heard Mum opening the door and then Martha's voice greeting her. I ran downstairs. We hugged each other, and then I dragged her into the living room and we just talked and talked. It was like seeing an old friend again, though I'd seen her only one brief time in Bangkok and then had stormed out of the room in a tantrum. We had a wonderful afternoon.

I was especially glad that Martha had made contact with Mum while I was in prison. Lucille had written to her as well, and I was grateful for every chance she had to meet Christians. I didn't want Mum to think that my own experiences were simply a reaction to the things that had happened to me in prison. After I became a Christian I prayed for her all the time. Because I was so happy and had found in the Lord Jesus everything for which my heart had been longing for so many years, I took it for granted that anybody who had it all explained to them simply would also grasp the offer of salvation with both hands.

So I sent Mum the booklet which had pointed me to God – Robert Laidlaw's *The Reason Why*[1] – and told her what had happened. She wrote back, obviously very happy at the change in me, but distressed at not being able to share my new-found faith.

'I do pray,' she wrote back to me. 'And what I pray is that God will bring you home.' It was the one thing she most prayed for, and in her letters I sensed with some sadness

---

1 Many readers of *Freed for Life* have asked me how they can obtain this booklet. It is now published by Send the Light, and can be ordered through any Christian bookshop or direct from STL Books, PO Box 48, Bromley, Kent.

that she was making a sort of condition – that unless God brought about my release, she would not think anything of him.

Now that I had been released, Mum was happy to share with me in everything. The next Sunday we went together to St. Andrew's Church, which was our local church. Once again, I enjoyed it enormously. The congregation was quite a big one, the singing was hearty, people were as friendly as could be; and though I didn't take in much of the sermon, I could certainly see that this church took the Bible seriously and talked about Jesus as a real person. Mum enjoyed it too, because it was a local church near her home, and she saw several people she knew there; it wasn't as if it was something new and intimidating, one of the intrusive consequences of the publicity I had attracted, but part of everyday Blackburn life. Brian Robinson, the vicar, made us welcome, and because the congregation was largely made up of our neighbours I didn't feel so conspicuous as I had the Sunday before.

So the problem I had worried about in Bangkok – how I was going to fit into a church in England and find people who really knew Jesus – was dealt with gently and painlessly by the Lord, and I was very grateful.

Going to church gave me a reference point. There I found my bearings. To hear other Christians talking about Jesus, and to sing hymns of praise and worship God in the serenity and beauty of worship, was a new experience; but it only enriched what I already knew. Perhaps that was why the Lord gave me a welcoming church so soon, to give me a secure foothold in the large world outside my family and my home.

I certainly needed it. Coming to terms with living in a town again was going to take time, and there was so much that I had either forgotten or was new since I had left home. I was especially disconcerted by television. Had it been so violent when I was last in England? The killings and shootings in the plays and films seemed so lifelike, and the evening news was full of pictures of heartbreaking deprivation and harrowing grief.

In all probability I had seen many similar things before I left home. But it all seemed different now; either because I hadn't got used to TV again, or because I had changed.

One evening I was sitting in Ann's house, watching a television thriller with her family. At one point I winced and looked away. Little Jonathan turned to me and said reassuringly, 'Don't worry, Auntie Rita. It's not real. It's only pretend, it's on the TV.'

I looked back at the screen. The scene was a prison cell. A prisoner was banging his head against a stone wall, monotonously, rhythmically striking his skull against the unyielding barrier.

'It's just pretend, you see?' Jonathan repeated.

In the cell, the prisoner continued his slow head-banging. His face was expressionless, his eyes showed no pain. The prison cell bore little resemblance to the wooden huts of Lard Yao, but the look on his face was familiar and authentic. I had seen similar mute misery on the faces of hundreds of people in prison, a language of despair that demanded no fluency in the Thai language in order to be read.

It's not pretend, it isn't at all, I whispered to myself. *I've seen it. And I thought I'd left it behind.*

5: Adjusting

The euphoria was beginning to fade.
Freed for Life, chapter 24

'You know, Rita,' remarked June one evening, after I'd been home for a few weeks, 'do you realise – you've never talked about what it was like, in prison?'

'You're right,' I admitted. 'It's awful; the fact is, I can't remember one thing about the place.'

It worried and distressed me. It was true; I found it almost impossible to remember much about Lard Yao. I'd been imprisoned in the place only weeks before. In my darkest moments there, I'd surveyed the prison bitterly and thought, *this place will never leave me.* I believed – we all believed – that the sights, the sounds, the smells of that place would be engraved on our memories for ever. We used to talk about it in the dormitories, the fear that our lives would always be scarred by the nightmare memories of what we had seen and experienced in prison, and the simple, horrifying fact that we had had our freedom taken away.

How could I ever forget it? In Lard Yao, I had laughed with murderers, talked to arsonists, and known scores of women who were drug addicts, drug dealers or convicted for crimes of violence.

And yet only a few days after returning home it had all gone. It was as if the prison, every detail of which I knew so well I could have found my way round it blindfolded, had been washed from my mind. All that was left was a hazy memory of shapes and voices, shadows hard to identify or put a name to.

I was bewildered and shamed by this experience. There were good friends of mine still in Bangkok, still in prison. Who was I to forget them? It was like a betrayal. And yet I had forgotten them, for though I remembered their names I could hardly put a face to any of them.

I talked to Mum about it.

'It's awful, Mum. It's gone, it's rubbed out. I just can't remember. Oh Mum, it's horrible – to have forgotten all that so quickly!'

Though I had forgotten many of the precise details, prison still cast a long shadow over my life and that of my family. Sleep was the least of my problems; I had a few troublesome nightmares, but they were not many. Though it was months before I could feel comfortable in a chair, I slept in a bed from the first night I came back to England. After the first few nights of scant slumber and much tossing and turning, I was quite quickly back into a reasonable sleep pattern. Neither did I continue to wear Eastern clothes, but adapted back to English ones with no problems – in fact it was hardly possible to do otherwise in the depths of the English winter.

Meals were a different matter. I tried to get used to the tastes of European food once again, but it was really hard. Mum cooked all sorts of treats for me, but I was plagued by stomach upsets. My system just wasn't used to that kind of food any more.

'I've made your favourite – potato pie,' she would say, and serve me with a normal-sized helping.

'Oh, lovely!' I would reply, and try my hardest to do it

justice. Mum and June would watch me apprehensively, and sure enough, after a few mouthfuls my stomach would begin to protest and I would push the plate away.

'I'm sorry, Mum, I just can't manage any more.'

For several weeks I couldn't finish a plateful of cooked food, and I could hardly touch fried food like bacon and eggs. Mum was at her wit's end. 'What *can* you manage, then?' she demanded.

'Could you make me some pea soup? Or some spare ribs?'

Mum tried hard to devise tasty and nourishing meals for me that wouldn't upset my digestive organs. Sometimes she was successful, but often I ended up spending half the day locked in the bathroom feeling like death. In the end we devised a routine that seemed to work. During the day I ate lots of fresh salad, and then in the evening I had a very tiny helping of whatever the others were eating. Mum always took the trouble to make something special, usually a dish that we'd enjoyed when I was small.

I enjoyed helping Mum with the cooking, even though I couldn't digest much of what resulted. All the ordinary, everyday household jobs were endlessly fascinating – it was all so new and different after prison. Going for walks on the moors was lovely, but I also enjoyed just walking down to the shops, seeing all the sights and sounds which I'd taken for granted before I left home and which now seemed very precious. Life was packed with all sorts of interesting things – watching TV, chatting with Mum and June and visitors, reading newspapers. Things which are now quite mundane to me were then totally absorbing, and life was very full.

'Aren't you bored?' I was asked. 'After all, you've just come back from a hair-raising experience, and you were a seasoned globe-trotter before that. Doesn't it drive you out of your mind, sitting here in your Mum's house with nothing to do?'

'Nothing to do?' I retorted. 'Why, there's shopping, talking to people, helping Mum —'

I think some people thought I was just making the best of a bad job and was staying home to be with my family out of consideration. But it wasn't true. When you've been in prison you learn not to be bored. I could be — and still can be — contented for hours, simply lying on my bed with my own thoughts. In prison you come to value time differently to how you did outside. Forced to be indoors early in the evening, one of the skills I developed in Lard Yao was to ignore everything going on around me and be at peace. So although it was unrealistic to expect Mum and June to spend every minute of every day looking after me and making sure I was being entertained, I never felt bored at all.

As I began to immerse myself in everyday life again, I began to be able to remember the details of prison life once more. At first it was like remembering a particularly vivid bad dream, when you remember less the characters in the dream than the feelings and fears you had while it was going on. Part of it, I think, was an unconscious unwillingness to face the fact that I was at home, wearing nice clothes, eating what I wanted to, free to do as I liked, while they were still locked away. It was some time before I could summon up their faces, recall their voices, allow them to be real people in my memory again.

I finally found myself able to remember Lard Yao, paradoxically, when walking the windy hills behind Mum's house. Striding up the slope, with Blackburn spread out like a well-trodden carpet below, I found myself remembering everything. It was as if someone had unlocked the doors of my memory. Suddenly I could recall faces and voices with sharp clarity: Hannah, Maria, Jenny, Chris, Linda, Mary and all the others. As the wind whipped my face, a wonderful warm feeling took hold of me as I thought of them, probably at that very moment stabbing bright scraps of cloth in the prison sewing factory or sitting on the grass chatting in the last half hour before the guards arrived for the evening lock-up. 'Lord, it will be like this for them one day,' I cried out. Then I turned back home and wrote long letters to them.

'Look,' I wrote, 'all the things we thought about that place, they go, you know? You never think you'll be free of it, ever again. But when you go out it leaves you. You'll be free too, you're coming out, so hold on, hold on . . .'

I don't know if it was helpful or not, but I had to say it because it was so real to me.

Perhaps if somebody had written me a letter like that in prison I'd have found it very hard to respond. The one thing you don't do in prison is dream about when you'll be released. Prison is such a vivid reality, dominating the full twenty-four hours of every day. You can't get out until you are out, not even in your mind. But nevertheless, I wanted to write these things to them, and over the months I wrote them to everyone I had known in prison.

'Wow, here's a letter from Bangkok!'

It was a morning in mid-February. I picked up the fat airmail envelope with its colourful stamps and opened it, to find a letter and two newspaper clippings.

It was from Lucille, a warm, joyous letter. I had been deeply sad at having to leave her so soon after greeting her in the British Embassy in Bangkok when I was released. For over two years she had visited me in prison. When she first began to visit me with Margaret Cole, another Christian to whom I had been grieved to say goodbye, I was sullen and bitterly resentful, as I was to everyone who spoke to me. Often Lucille had queued for two hours to see me in Lard Yao only to find that I refused to talk or that I was being forbidden visiting privileges because of some real or imagined misdoings. When I met her at the Embassy it was the first time I had spoken to her without an iron grille between us – the first time I had been able to hug her. It had been an all-too-brief meeting, because I was being expelled from Thailand and had to leave the country almost immediately after leaving prison.

So a letter from Lucille brought back many memories. The most wonderful and joyful memory, however, was prompted by the newspaper clippings. They were from Bangkok newspapers, both dated February 5, and both told the same story.

> In a surprise decision which overruled verdicts of the Criminal and Appeals Court, the Dika (Supreme) Court yesterday set free a Spanish woman who was earlier sentenced to 40 years in jail on a drug trafficking charge . . . The Dika Court dropped charges, deciding that she was innocent and was not connected with the trafficking of 15,995 grammes of heroin found in her possession more than two years ago.

From the clippings the face of Maria looked at me; hair cropped short, clothes crumpled, her face tired and harrassed. But it was Maria, and she had been set free.

'Whatever's the matter?' Mum asked in concern. 'Bad news?'

'No, Mum, it's good news, it's really good news . . .' I pushed the clippings into her hand. I wasn't able to say any more. Mum was moved too. She had heard all about Maria from my letters, and had followed the ups and downs of her story. I'd told her since of my anguish at leaving Maria in her cell, where she had become withdrawn and dirty, almost certainly deeply scarred mentally and emotionally. She was my mother's age, and we had been very close.

When I had pressed my face to the bars of her dark and smelly cell, trying to persuade her to recognise me so I could say goodbye, it was the one desperately unhappy aspect of my release. That was why I had been so upset by seeing her featured in the centre pages of the *Daily Mail*. Now I was seeing her story again in another newspaper, but what a different story it had become!

I looked at the clippings again. They said that the decision had been made because the Court had not been prepared to accept evidence from the two main witnesses, as they directly contradicted each other. 'Surprise decision' – yes, it certainly was. In the dormitory in Lard Yao many of us had discussed her case for nights on end, and none of us had thought there was ever going to be any chance of the verdict being quashed. I fleetingly remembered the agony of deciding which of us would have to tell her what the Court's verdict had been – we gave Hannah the task in the end, and she had found it next to impossible to make her understand. Eventually Maria's consular visitors had explained to her in her own language. At that time the official reports on the radio said that she had been given a life sentence.

'They called my release "unique", Mum, and now they've called Maria's "a surprise decision". Oh, Mum, they don't understand – it's God, do you see? He made it possible. He answered all those prayers . . . .'

I was especially anxious to find out more about Maria's whereabouts. I didn't have the address of the Spanish officials out there, so I just addressed a letter to 'The Spanish Embassy, Bangkok', asking if they could give me any information.

I didn't hear anything from them, so I wondered whether I could contact her any other way. A friend in London who knew Spanish offered to write to her for me at the address she'd given me in Lard Yao, but I decided that wouldn't be right – I wasn't sure what mental state she would be in, and I didn't want to contact her through a stranger. I wanted to see her more than anything. We were beginning to talk about going away for a family holiday in Spain, and I thought I might possibly be able to get to Madrid and somehow find her.

But all my enquiries led nowhere, and eventually I had to give up and trust the Lord that wherever Maria was, she was happy and cared for.

Money was a recurring problem, though Mum never mentioned it. She had retired while I was in prison, and though not yet at retirement age she had her widow's pension, and was living on that. Though she didn't have a job her days were always full – she visited Auntie Mary every day, for example. Her sore shoulder stopped her from doing anything strenuous, but she was active and involved in quite a number of different things locally.

I was concerned that my arrival had put a strain on the household finances. At first it was fine, because when I came home I was given several gifts of money, about £200 altogether, and I was also given the residue of some money that had been collected by public appeal while I was in Bangkok; most of it had been used to promote my case and publicise my innocence, but there was a lump sum left when I came home.

I bought myself some things I needed, and some small presents for family and friends. The rest I put aside, and out of it gave Mum some money for my upkeep each week. But I knew it wouldn't last for ever. It wouldn't be fair then to live off Mum; she had no savings and her pension wasn't enough for two to live on. June was working, and was contributing her share of the household expenses. I felt I would be doing the same. I had to do something, and one evening we had a long talk about it.

'We'd better talk to the Employment Exchange,' said Mum. 'Find out what you're entitled to. There must be something.'

We went to the Department of Health and Social Security in Blackburn. I was interviewed by an efficiently friendly Social Security officer.

'What attempts have you made to find employment?'

'None,' I said apologetically. 'You see I've just . . .'

'You must understand,' said the officer sharply, 'that any benefit paid to you while unemployed is only paid on the basis that you are actively looking for work.'

However, when we explained the situation to her, she was immediately understanding. 'Naturally it will take some time for you to readjust. We have discretion in these cases,' she told us, 'to make a temporary hardship grant. It means that you will receive a single lump sum payment to cover your present needs.' She flipped through a file of notes. 'Now, presumably you will be in a position to start looking for work in due course.'

I nodded.

'I'm afraid that you are not eligible for Unemployment Benefit, as you were last working outside this country. But you are eligible for Supplementary Benefit.'

She put a form in front of me. 'Will you fill that in, please. You'll be notified in due course.'

Afterwards I wondered again what I ought to do about looking for a job. I considered resuming my nursing training, but wasn't sure how to go about it. Also I had a dominent idea in my mind that somehow, somewhere, I would be working with prisoners. *After what I've been through, there has to be some way I can help people who are like I was*, I reflected. Perhaps the Probation Service? I didn't want to be a 'do-gooder', but involved in some practical way. Various possibilities sounded interesting, but I was determined to think hard about them. I wasn't going to rush headlong into things. That was how I'd got into trouble last time.

When the notification came through from the

Department of Social Security I found that I had been awarded Supplementary Benefit of £17 a week. Out of it I was able to give Mum money for my keep, though she was always reluctant to accept it.

It was strange to have a regular income again. I'd come back to an England which had a grave unemployment problem, and I knew that when I began to look for work I would find it difficult. A working knowledge of the Thai language and the ability to dance and chat with visitors to night clubs were not very impressive qualifications when job-hunting in Lancashire! But now at least I had a small income.

In Lard Yao I had sometimes wondered what it would be like to have a salary again, and what my attitude should be to money as a Christian. When I had been home a few weeks, Brian, the vicar at St. Andrew's, preached a sermon about how Christians should handle their money. He spoke about giving. It was a very direct sermon.

'When you give away a few pennies that you didn't need anyway, it's not *my* problem,' he said. 'But what does God think about it? Is that the sort of giving that he talks about in the Bible?'

Sitting with my Mum I remembered the Bible passages I'd read, about how we ought to give freely to God because he has given so freely to us. All that we have comes from him. All that we have belongs to him. It's a privilege, said Brian, to be able to give out of what God has given us.

That's what I must do, I decided, as the sermon came to an end. From that Sunday on, I put part of my weekly income into the collection at St. Andrew's.

As I grew more in the Christian life and read more books and met more Christians I found out about 'tithing', and it made a lot of sense to me. But I'd already acquired the habit of giving one tenth of my income to God. It wasn't an intellectual decision reached after careful consideration of the relevant Bible texts. It was a spontaneous response to what God had done for me in those weeks after coming home. I don't think I was ever so blessed in my life as when I first came back to England. I wanted to share it. In the middle of such happiness and joy, giving seemed the most natural thing in the world. And I can certainly testify to the fact that I've never been poor, I've never starved, and God has given me far more than I have ever given back to him. I would recommend any Christian to consider what the Bible says about tithing. It could open up a whole new dimension of the Christian life!

6: Shadows

*To some it may have seemed odd that I could
stand up before total strangers and proclaim
my faith, while with my own family I was
sometimes faltering, always reticent. I didn't
understand it myself. I like to think it was
the guidance of the Spirit urging boldness at
one point and caution at another. More
likely, as a new Christian I was just making
the bucketful of mistakes which all excited
freshmen believers do.*

Charles W. Colson, *Born Again* (1977),
chapter 14

Mum's sore shoulder wasn't getting any better, despite
several visits to the doctor. One day when it seemed to be
bothering her more than usual, I couldn't stand watching
her in pain any more.

'Mum, whatever's the matter with your arm? You look
really uncomfortable.'

She shook her head and wriggled her shoulder
experimentally. 'It's such a nuisance, Rita. It's been like it
for ages. I've had this ache for twelve months or more.' She
winced and cradled her shoulder in a brief twinge of pain.

Suddenly I was really concerned. 'Twelve months? You

should see a doctor, Mum. Get it sorted out. You shouldn't be in pain for that long, it isn't right.'

Mum shrugged. 'I did – months ago. They gave me some painkillers. They didn't work all that well, so they gave me some other ones. If they've tried me on one kind they've tried me on a dozen. They say now they think it's arthritis and want me to have physiotherapy.' She frowned fretfully. '*More* running around. I've got to get it X-rayed first. As if I'd got time for all that.'

Outside some kids were playing. Distant screams and laughter floated through the window. For a minute or two Mum sat nursing her shoulder, and I sat watching her. There wasn't much I could do. I reached out a hand to rub her back, but Mum got to her feet and smiled. 'I'll make us a cup of tea, Rita.'

'Let me, Mum,' I said. She shook her head.

'Exercise, that's what this arm of mine needs. That's what they told me.' She went through to the kitchen. 'Fat lot of good it does,' she added.

I began to pray about Mum's shoulder. I added it to a list of things I was praying about. After the first week or so of disorientation I had got back into a routine of regularly reading the Bible and talking to God, thinking through the next few days with him and asking him for his help, and bringing various matters to him that I wanted to specially talk to him about.

I found it helpful to read my Bible at the same time each day, just as I'd done in prison. Sometimes it wasn't possible to do so, and I don't believe at all that it's catastrophic if a Christian can't always read a certain amount of the Bible at a set time each day (though it can be very helpful, especially when you're just starting out in the Christian life). We're told to feed on God's Word and let it be a light to us, but deciding how we're going to make it part of our lives is an individual choice.

For myself, I always read the Bible in bed in the morning, before I got up. Mum was a much earlier riser than I was and she'd usually been up and about for a while. She used to bring me a cup of tea in bed. Gwen Abbott, who had regularly sent me a series of Bible notes called *Every Day with Jesus* when I was in Lard Yao, continued to send them to me in Blackburn after I got home, and I found it very helpful to have a guide to what I was reading to make me think, and explain the difficult bits or the parts that had to do with life in first-century Palestine.

In prison, I'd been sent a book called *God Calling, by Two Listeners*, and discovered to my delight that Mum had also been sent a copy. In our letters, we discovered that we'd both been reading it – it was a devotional booklet, arranged in passages for each day – and we began to quote it to each other, often just mentioning the date. It was a little like Maria and myself reading our respective Bibles, pointing out the chapter and verse numbers to each other so we could look them up and read them. 'Remember Tuesday's words?' Mum might write to me, and I'd know exactly what she meant. It had been lovely to think of us both getting excited about the same things and underlining the same words, but it was even better now I was home and we could sit together in the same room with the book.

In fact, when I first got home, I had no books. I'd had a copy of *Daily Light* in Bangkok which Lucille had given me, but that and my Bible had been left by accident in an Embassy car and I only got them back after several months had passed. So I borrowed Mum's Bible and her copy of *God Calling*. I was thrilled to see that she had been reading it and marking the bits she'd enjoyed.

I found praying strange at first. For so long I'd prayed for one thing in particular, and that was my release. Now it had happened. It wasn't exactly an anti-climax, but I found it hard to adjust to laying my daily life before the Lord without that single, over-riding plea to crown all my other thanks and requests. I found it easy to read a bit of the Bible and enjoy the good things I found there, and then leap out of bed and get dressed and rush off to do exciting things. Then later on in the day I would think, *Oh, I didn't have my prayer-time this morning, I didn't talk to God.* Then I'd excuse myself by saying how busy I was and how exciting everything was that day. But often I would find myself thinking, *But he's never too busy to speak to you . . .* So that evening I'd try to make time to talk to him longer.

The Lord was really gentle with me in those first weeks. I've heard many Christians say that if they don't have a proper prayer-time first thing in the day then nothing goes right, and they know that something's badly wrong. But God was very good to me. He let me have my bubbly time and settle down at my own pace, and he gently reminded me when I had neglected to talk to him, and when I prayed to him it was as if I'd never wandered away.

The transition from prison to home was a difficult one spiritually, because in so many ways I had had extraordinary experiences as a Christian, and yet I was ignorant of so much. I had lived a solitary, lonely life in Lard Yao, with only a few Christians to help me. Now I had to take my part in the family of God's people, as part of a local church congregation. The prospect was thrilling but a little frightening as well.

Looking back on my prison experiences I sometimes thought of them as almost a honeymoon time, when my relationship with God was uniquely intimate and revolved around very special demonstrations of his goodness to me. Each new book of the Bible I read was like a new jewel I'd discovered, and every aspect of the Christian faith gleamed as if it was brand-new and I the first who had ever encountered it. I'm sure God would like us to be like that all the time, and I'm sure he forgives us when we're not. In my case, I simply found it all too easy to stop depending on him. That was how I'd got into tantrums at the Stirk House Hotel, but at least there I had some sort of excuse because I was exhausted and over-excited. Now, back in a more everyday routine, I was alarmed to find myself showing signs of spiritual laziness. When I'd prayed to God for my daily bread in prison, it had been a prayer of real need. Money from the Social Security was just as much a gift of God, but I found it hard to see it in quite the same way.

Fortunately I didn't have to sort out all these problems on my own. I had the church to help me, and as the weeks went by I came to value that church more and more as I realised how much I'd missed in Lard Yao.

To begin with we just went on Sundays, usually the morning service and sometimes the evening one as well. At first I felt that that was enough. It was all so new and exciting, and I wanted to take things slowly. But St. Andrew's was a welcoming church, which didn't let bystanders remain on the fringe of things for very long, and we were soon drawn into the life of the church.

In a strange way I resented becoming so involved. I felt that I wanted to set my own pace, to feel my way back into things; and I didn't want others pulling me along faster than I cared for. I wanted to be with my family, not pushed into other situations. I went to church to worship God, I told myself, not to get tangled up in telling everybody where I'd been and what had happened to me.

But then, as I began to go to the Thursday night Bible studies, I realised I'd been silly. On Sunday everybody had been very friendly and we'd really enjoyed being there, but it had been a formal service with people disappearing after church to make sure their lunch wasn't burning in the oven. Thursday nights were quite different, a time of relaxed fellowship where we began to get to know people properly and study the Bible together as fellow-Christians. In Lard Yao I'd led Bible studies, but there I'd been the 'mature

Christian', helping other people to understand. Now I was part of a small group, with some who were much older in the faith than I was and some who were much younger. We learned together, and talked about what we were learning, and for the first time I began to understand what 'Christian fellowship' really meant.

Mum often came to the Thursday evening meetings with me, and she enjoyed it just as much as I did. I didn't say very much, and I appreciated the fact that the group didn't push me in any way. They knew my situation, and as time went by I frequently asked the group to pray for me as different things were happening and various decisions had to be made. But they never pushed me to give talks at the church or give my testimony.

The group was sometimes led by the vicar and sometimes by the curate, Herrick Daniels, a West Indian. Later it met in Herrick's house, and we got to know each other very well. He became a very special person in my life, and he helped me in scores of ways. I came to value his advice very much indeed. Mum liked him, too, and he was a great help to her.

I'd always known, since I became a Christian, that studying the Bible was important. But it took on a new meaning in that group, as we shared our experiences and read the Bible together.

The Bible study at St. Andrew's wasn't the only regular commitment I had to a Christian group. My other involvement came about as the result of a surprise visit from somebody I didn't know.

As my memories of people I'd known in prison came flooding back, so did my desire, first experienced in Lard Yao, to find a way to do something with my freedom which would help prisoners not just in Bangkok but world-wide. I began to pray that God would show me how this might happen. In prison I'd made a commitment to help other people in prisons once I myself was free. The newspapers had picked it up. I'd shared the hope with people in my family and in church. But how could I actually *do* it?

Several weeks after I came home I was sitting on my own one evening when there was a knock on the door.

'Hello, I'm Mary Thomas.'

I asked my visitor in, wondering who she was.

'I came to ask you whether you would be interested in coming to a prayer meeting. It's to pray for people in prison.'

I was immediately interested, and readily agreed to go. 'Yes, I'd love to come!'

The prayer meeting was at Preston, which is near Blackburn. It was held in a Baptist church where twenty or so people from different backgrounds had gathered to pray for different aspects of the prison work. Mary introduced me to the group with the minimum of fuss, and we began to pray. Individual prisoners were prayed for by name, and obviously the group had prayed for them before and knew a good deal about each of them. *It was groups like this that prayed for me when I was in Lard Yao*, I realised.

I began to pray aloud with them, talking about people I knew in Bangkok, for prisoners and for the Christians involved in visiting there, like Jack and Gladys Martin. It was a very poignant experience. I'd prayed at St. Andrews for my friends in prison; but there I was, in the middle of this group which had been praying for *me* while I was in Bangkok.

Afterwards we had coffee and biscuits, and I browsed among some leaflets at the back of the room and found some Prison Christian Fellowship literature. It was then that I realised that this was one of the regional prayer groups of the Fellowship. I was excited, and asked lots of questions, and took away with me a form to fill in and send to the London office for further details. I had an immediate reply, saying that the Fellowship had been wanting to make contact with me, having been in touch with the American

Fellowship – I remembered Sylvia Mary Alison's letter which I'd never answered. I became a regular member of the monthly prayer group and it was a way of keeping my commitment to prisoners while I waited for the Lord to show me the next step. I'd discovered how good it was to join in with the life of the church, and how important it was to be part of a fellowship of Christian believers, to share with them and learn from them. But there was another aspect of living as a Christian. Just as I couldn't expect to hide in my family and avoid committing myself to sharing in the life of the church, so I couldn't expect to take refuge in numbers and just be a Christian at church. If Christianity was truly a total change in my life, then that change must affect my life at home with my family.

From my first arrival home I had found it easy to talk about my new faith. I've always been an outgoing sort of person anyway, and I was so full of gratitude and excitement that it all flowed readily as I talked with my family.

I've never felt that I should preach to my relatives. We've not been the sort of family that talks very deeply about our religious beliefs anyway. But becoming a Christian was part of what had happened while I was away, so I was able to talk about it a great deal as I chatted about my experiences abroad generally. I talked a lot about what it meant to me to have given my life to Jesus, just as I'd written a lot about it in my letters from prison. But I didn't feel it right to argue with other people, whoever they were, and demand that they should become Christians there and then. I tried to share Jesus with them naturally and I prayed for them continually.

When I was a little girl, before my tenth birthday, I often went with Ann to stay with my Auntie Margaret and her husband (June was then too small to be away from home overnight). I remember that every night Auntie Margaret prayed with us, and that was something we never did at home. As I grew up she was always within reach, never saying much about Christianity; a gentle, caring aunt whom we all loved – as indeed all our aunts were loved. But I had a special relationship with her, because she was my Godmother, and I always thought of her as different.

Auntie Margaret listened quietly as I talked about what had happened to me in prison, occasionally asking the sort of questions that mean that the person asking them really understands what you're talking about. One day, after I'd been home for a while, she and I were talking together when she told me that many years ago she too had become a Christian.

'But it's always been for me a very private matter,' she said. 'I've never talked much about what it means to me.' She smiled. 'I'm really thrilled for you, Rita. I'm going to talk a bit more about what I believe from now on.'

I was so happy for her; and I had another wonderful surprise to come.

My Auntie Mary was another much-loved aunt. When I was in prison and Ann and June flew out to visit me, they brought bad news about her. She was seriously ill, so ill that John (Ann's husband) had advised them to tell me that she had already died; she wasn't expected to live for more than a few days, and it would have been better for me to hear it from them than by a letter after they had gone. In the end they told me the facts, that she was dreadfully ill and wasn't expected to recover. I had been heartbroken, not just because she was my Auntie but because I desperately wanted to talk to her about Jesus before she died.

So I prayed unceasingly for her and I know that many other people did; and not long after I heard that she had made a miraculous recovery. When I came home, it was wonderful to see her again, and she was a frequent visitor at home in Blackburn just as she had always been. One day she too told me that she had made a commitment to God many years ago. For her it was a joyful surprise to find her wayward, worldly niece coming home a Christian. For my part, it was lovely to come home to find two Christian aunts, though it was several months before they were able to share their faith with me fully.

There is no doubt that God blessed me by giving me the family he did. I know of many Christians living in homes where Christianity is ridiculed and where they suffer appalling hostility. Some who have become Christians in prison return to bitter criticism and contempt. I came home from Lard Yao to find nothing but love and understanding, and I was overwhelmed.

I hope that my family saw a dramatic change in my life, but I had been away from home for quite a long time, even before my arrest; so I don't know whether they ascribed any changes in lifestyle to that or to the fact that I was now a Christian. I went to church regularly, of course, and there was always a Bible lying around the house, but in other ways our family life wasn't altered.

I think that I feared that all the publicity, which had made a good deal of reference to my conversion, might make people think that I was going to come home as a Bible-thumping ranter, intent on bludgeoning everyone within reach into becoming Christians. I so much wanted my family and friends to share my new faith that I deliberately kept a low profile, saying what I could when I could, and praying very much that the Lord would not let me fail when opportunities came (as they often did) to explain, simply and clearly, exactly what it was that God had done in my life.

That was why I had reacted against the journalist who had promised to write about my 'religious experience'. I didn't want to be seen as a fanatic, somebody whose faith shone as the pinnacle and crown of her life – a 'religious' person. I desperately wanted my Christian beliefs to be seen as part and parcel of my whole life, not a separate commodity to be cultivated on its own and thrust before people willy-nilly. I believed in evangelism, I still believe in it; sharing my faith is vitally important to me. But I walked with care for the first few months of my return, and the Lord blessed me with the knowledge that others really understood what he had done for me.

Though we didn't pray at mealtimes as a family, we did pray together. The first time we did so was when I was sitting with Mum and Auntie Mary and Auntie Margaret discussing a family problem. It was something we were all concerned about and we didn't know what to do for the best. We'd been going over various alternatives and none had seemed helpful.

We sat staring at the teapot for a while, thinking. Then I plucked up my courage.

'Why don't we pray about it? I'll pray for all of us, if you like.' So I prayed, and it wasn't so terrifying as I'd thought.

After that first time it became much easier, and we prayed together quite often. It was never a forced or formal act, but flowed naturally from the situation we were in at the time.

I prayed with Mum, too, on my own; but that was less relaxed.

'I don't know, Rita, I haven't got faith like you.'

'What do you mean, Mum?'

'Uh – well, I'm not good enough to be a Christian.'

'Oh, Mum, that's not what it's about at all. Being a Christian hasn't got anything to do with whether you're good enough to be one. It's because of what Jesus has done for us. He did all that's needed.'

Such conversations were quite frequent in the first weeks of my return and they were frustrating in the extreme. I used to agonise for hours afterwards. How could she miss the point like that.?

'I did ask Jesus into my life once, Rita; I really did. But it doesn't seem real to me, somehow. I don't feel it. I'm not good enough, that's what it is . . .'

For a few weeks I tried to argue her out of it, and took every chance of explaining why she was wrong and what the Bible said, but I began to realise that I was only building up resentment and making Mum feel guilty. So I stopped that, and I just handed over the whole problem to the Lord. I went to church with her and talked with her about what we'd heard when I could. I tried very hard to stand back and let the Holy Spirit do what he wished in Mum's life. It was difficult to let go. I wouldn't have let go at all, had I not known that the Lord Jesus knew all about the situation.

7: Living Forwards

*I'm praying for guidance and he's giving it
to me. He's not going to let me down
now – he's guided me this far.*

Jubilee, March 1980

The slightly built man in the immaculate suit beamed at
Mum. Mum repeated what she'd just said. He turned to
Ann, his face wrinkling with amusement.

'Please, what is Momma saying?'

Mum giggled, Ann attempted to translate, but Mr. Goehr
smiled at Mum and said genially, 'No, I understand. But
Momma must talk a little slower. Then it will be fine.'

She slowed down for him, and measured her words
carefully, but after a few sentences she was back in full flow
and Mr. Goehr had to bring Ann in as translator. When a
Blackburn resident gets into his or her vocal stride it can be
a problem for those from other parts of the country to keep
up; and Mr. Goehr, whose English was impeccable and
precise, was no exception.

We were having a wonderful time. Mr. Goehr was a
distinguished consultant on international law who had done
a tremendous amount of work on my behalf while I was in
prison. He would take no payment for this, and our family

were deeply grateful to him. A few days after I arrived home a crate of champagne had arrived at Mum's house with a message of congratulations from him.

Mr. Goehr's card had a message promising that he would be in touch with us in due course, but it was an unexpected surprise when his invitation arrived six weeks later: he invited us to have lunch with him in London.

Mum, Ann and her baby Emma, and I went down to London on the train and met Mr. Goehr at his office. It was an emotional meeting for Mum and Ann, because he'd been very supportive and had encouraged them while all the anxiety and waiting was going on. I thought he looked quite like I remembered my father; a dapper, pleasant-looking man with greying hair, very distinguished and with a lovely kind expression in his eyes. After the greetings he and his assistant took us to a very grand restaurant, and we lunched on oysters, smoked salmon and other delicacies.

Before we said goodbye he took me on one side and talked to me on my own, and I had an opportunity to tell him how much we appreciated what he'd done. But truth to tell, I never will know all he did, just as I will never know more than a fraction of the efforts that many people made in securing my release. I do know that he made a special effort to protect Mum from a lot of the legal paperwork and similar worries, and so I have a special gratitude for him. There wasn't time to say much to him then, but I was so glad to have met him after knowing so much about him.

We walked down Piccadilly and on to the Foreign Office. The London theatres were closed, because it was lunchtime, and the neon signs were lifeless skeletons in the spring sunshine. Here and there were the entrances to night clubs, with gaudy signs and garishly coloured photographs pinned on boards outside. Although the red London buses and the English shopfronts made the scene familiar and known, I couldn't help remembering the Hong Kong clubs, the faded plush entrance of the Kokasai where I'd been a hostess and all my problems had started. It seemed a remote, distant world.

Into my mind came the memory of a disco I'd been to with June a few weeks earlier in Blackburn, and the terrible sadness I'd felt as I watched the dancers strutting up and down, men predatory for women, women predatory for men, and all the other things I'd seen every night in Hong Kong. In that northern disco I had realised, probably for the first time, what it means when the Bible talks about people being lost without God. *People are looking, looking for what they don't find, and they never will find it. I know, because I looked for it all over the world.*

I broke out of my reverie as we walked into Whitehall and the massive edifice of the Foreign Office. Mr. Southworth, who'd been so kind to me in Bangkok, knew we were coming, and he welcomed us and introduced us to some of the people who'd been involved in my case. As a special treat we were allowed a glimpse of an enormous pile of folders, all of which apparently were to do with my arrest and imprisonment. I knew that my arrest had caused a great deal of work in official quarters; to see the documentation was very impressive.

On the train home we enthused over Mr. Goehr's hospitality and reminisced about the long struggle for my release. Ann, who had been the family spokesman to the press and whose husband John had also been involved in keeping public interest in my plight going, told me several parts of the story I didn't know, having been isolated in Bangkok. All in all, it was a day which reinforced as nothing else could, my gratitude to so many people who had refused to let my problems be ignored.

At Easter we went on a family holiday to Spain, where we relaxed and enjoyed the break from what had been, all in all, an exhausting few months. We lazed on the beach and went for walks around historic parts of the resort, ate at exotic restaurants and had a lovely time. Mum in particular looked as if she really could do with a rest. The doctor had put her on a different course of tablets, and she was having heat treatment for her shoulder. She looked grey and tired, and the holiday seemed to do her good. Looking at her sometimes I caught myself thinking, *It doesn't seem fair, she's had to go through such a lot – and now this on top.*

I tried to find out where Maria was, and made a few enquiries in local government offices, but had no success. By the time we left Spain I'd heard nothing, and I have heard nothing from her since. I pray for her regularly, and I hope that one day we will meet up again.

When we got home we all felt better for the break. We got back into the routine of church and local events, and somehow, having been abroad again and back in a short time, I felt much more at home in Blackburn – I'd lost the feeling of 'just got back from Thailand' and replaced it with the feeling of 'just been away from home for a couple of weeks'. The local people still occasionally stared in the street, but I didn't mind.

By now Mum had been put on a course of physiotherapy for her arm and shoulder which were still giving her a lot of pain. But we still went to church together, and by now Mum wasn't just 'Rita's mum', tagging along after me, but a member of the group in her own right. She didn't say much at the Thursday Bible studies – neither did I – but she listened very carefully to all that went on, and from time to time I had the opportunity to discuss things with her and sometimes answer questions she had.

Then one Thursday night we came home from the Bible study and Mum was rather quiet. I flopped into an armchair and Mum came into the lounge after me. Without any fuss she remarked, 'I really asked Jesus into my life tonight.'

She was abrupt, matter-of-fact; I stared at her, not quite taking in what she'd said.

'I asked him into my life, Rita.' She gazed at me and I at her. She blinked. 'Share with me again, Rita. Tell me what it means, me making that decision. Go over it with me.'

With my heart bursting with love and thanks to the Lord Jesus I showed her what the Bible says about becoming a Christian. I carefully explained, in a way that I had not done with Mum for weeks, how it wasn't a matter of her *doing* anything, but of God loving her so much that he sent his Son, Jesus, to die for her. 'All you have to do is to believe, Mum — have faith that he loves us, and ask him to save you.'

There was a moment's silence and then Mum looked at me bright-eyed. 'That's what I did, Rita. I did that tonight. It's real, I know it's right.'

The joy of knowing that Mum had become a Christian lit up my life. It was a time when I was very aware of God working. Several things were happening which made me realise that the Lord was very specially directing my life step-by-step.

I went to London for a few days to visit Gwen Abbott. It was hard to leave Mum. She was very distressed when we said goodbye.

'You're going away again, Rita.'

'Mum, it's only London — only a few days. I'll ring you every night. I promise.'

As the train started on its journey south I was haunted by the picture of Mum's set, wan face, smiling bravely as her slight figure receded into the distance and merged into the formless mass of people on the station platform.

While I was in London I had a telephone call.

'My name's Ross Simpson,' said a friendly voice. 'I'm ringing on behalf of Prison Christian Fellowship.'

'Oh!' I said. I dimly recalled the name from Prison Christian Fellowship literature. I wondered what could be his reason for calling.

'Mr. Colson is in London at the moment,' he explained,

'and he has said that he would very much like to meet you. Would you be free to meet him over dinner?'

'Of course! When?'

I was delighted. Chuck Colson represented for me somebody who had actually chosen to work among prisoners and had founded an organisation to make this possible, and I admired him tremendously.

'We would love you to meet us at Gilbert Kirby's house. He is the principal of London Bible College and is entertaining Mr. Colson and some of the staff there on April 21. Can you come?'

'I'll certainly be there,' I promised.

Gilbert Kirby and his wife Connie lived in a large, comfortable modern house attached to the College in North London. About ten people had been invited, but the dining room was big, so we were able to relax and enjoy a delicious meal, talking all the time. When I arrived I was welcomed by Mr. Kirby – I hadn't expected the principal of a Bible College to be such a friendly, homely person – and introduced to Ross Simpson and John Harris. John was six feet tall, with distinguished grey hair and spectacles. He greeted me in a jolly, booming voice that fitted his height. I liked him on sight, as I did Ross, another very tall man who was most excited because that day his wife had had a baby. Both men were relaxed and amusing to be with. Chuck Colson wasn't there yet as he was coming from a meeting elsewhere. So I had a chance to sit with John and Ross and get to know them.

They were full of enthusiasm for the way that God was blessing the work of Prison Christian Fellowship, and told me many encouraging things. I was moved that people had prayed for so long for prisoners, and had a vision of working with them. I was so absorbed in talking with John and Ross that by the time Chuck Colson appeared I'd relaxed enough to forget my shyness.

He arrived with Gordon and Beth Loux, his associates in

Prison Fellowship USA. I was surprised how tall he was. Prison Fellowship seemed to attract large men! He had the most extraordinary face, expressive eyes that looked straight at you, and mobile, well-used features which seemed to reflect every changing mood and thought. Talking to Chuck you get the feeling that he holds nothing back. Meeting him for the first time, I felt completely at ease with him.

His wife Patty, who I'd met in her husband's books, was lovely. She hugged me and sat down with me, and we were soon in animated conversation. I suppose I had thought that the wife of somebody so important as Chuck Colson would have been remote and inaccessible, but neither of them were like that.

'I'm sure glad to meet you, after all this time,' said Chuck warmly. 'People ask me about you wherever I go, all over.'

He talked to me about Kathryn Grant's visit to me in Bangkok, how she had reported back that it was a terribly sad situation and a bleak prospect for the future, but that I was happy and contented in the Lord. And then I'd been suddenly released. When I made my telephone call to the Fellowship offices from the Stirk House Hotel, they'd been praying for me at a staff prayer meeting minutes before.

'You should come to the States,' Chuck remarked. 'See the work at first hand, how we do things. We'd love to have you come over.'

I shook my head. 'It's not the right time just now,' I answered regretfully. 'My mum's not very well, and anyway I still feel as if I've only just got back. I oughtn't to go away at present.'

Chuck nodded sympathetically.

'But,' I added impulsively, 'I am really interested in the work. I don't want to lose touch.'

'We won't lose touch,' promised Chuck.

During the evening many things were talked about, and for much of the time I listened entranced, not contributing anything because I wasn't familiar with the situations they were talking about. The picture that emerged was of a group of people in several different parts of the world who shared Chuck's vision of Christians taking the message of the gospel into prisons, sharing the good news in seminars and small groups, and inspiring local Christians to meet together and pray for prisoners, giving them help and support in whatever ways presented themselves.

I learned that John Harris and Ross Simpson had been associated with Prison Christian Fellowship in England since its earliest days, when Sylvia Mary Alison had invited them to join a prayer group which was looking to God for guidance about the formation of the work. John's base was now the London office, and Ross, who was a senior probation officer, was an unpaid worker who travelled around the country visiting local groups and encouraging the work there. It wasn't a very grand organisation, and the staff were few. The Fellowship's priorities, just like those of the American organisation, were to concentrate its resources on building up a network of praying, caring Christians and on getting its representatives into the prisons to share the gospel with prisoners.

I was able to talk with Chuck for a long time, and he told me how widespread had been the concern and prayer for my release. I learned that there had been groups of people formed for the particular purpose of praying for me.

'One day you must come to America,' he reminded me. 'There are so many people who would love to meet you. You have a lot of friends there.'

Afterwards I wondered when it would happen. I'd been in touch by letter with the American Fellowship staff since my return, and Kathryn had raised the question of a visit. I really wanted to go, and I'd been praying about it.

But it was entirely the wrong time. Mum was looking tired and washed out, and the treatment on her shoulder didn't seem to be helping her at all. There was no way I was going to travel abroad until Mum was better. It would have been unfair to leave her. So I wrote to Kathryn, explaining that I couldn't think about going to America just yet, but that I wanted to go later on; then I put the matter out of my mind and concentrated on my family.

8: Mum

*Months of raised hopes and shattered dreams
had failed to daunt the courageous woman
who witnessed her daughter's distress, first-
hand during a visit to Thailand. During the
months of waiting, Lily's spirit never
faltered. She'd have done battle with the
whole government if it could have brought
Rita home earlier.*

The Guardian, 5 February 1981

The next few weeks were a lovely time of sharing Mum's
happiness as she began to rest in the security of her new-
found faith in Jesus. Our churchgoing was transformed,
and Herrick Daniels in particular spent a lot of time with
her. Mum was very quiet about what had happened – she
wasn't somebody who went around speaking her feelings to
everybody – but you could see in her face that something
had happened.

Sadly, her joy had to compete with her pain. Even with
heat treatment and exercise, she didn't improve.

I found myself very confused about it. *Lord, what are you
doing?* I prayed. *Mum's given her life to you. She loves you.
Why isn't it for her like it was for me? Why don't you take
away her pain?* I prayed earnestly and often, and talked to

friends about it, and was given wise counsel, but none of it really answered my questions. I sat with her, reading the Bible with her, praying with her; all the time looking at her when her attention was distracted, looking uneasily at the worn face and the awkward positions she was having to adopt in order not to put her shoulder under stress.

Then one day she stayed in bed. It was the May Bank Holiday, and we were all going to Blackpool for a day out. I went into Mum's bedroom to see what the matter was. She was lying in bed, staring bleakly at the wall.

'Why, Mum whatever's wrong? You look dreadful!'

'I'm ill, Rita,' she said wearily. 'I'm not so well at all.'

I felt her brow. She seemed very unwell indeed. I plumped up her pillows and tried to make her more comfortable.

'I won't go to Blackpool, Mum. I'll stay home and look after you.'

'Oh, don't do that, you go on to Blackpool,' Mum said weakly. 'I feel too weak to be bothered with anyone.'

I thought for a minute. Maybe Mum was right. She'd been overdoing it and her shoulder had been really sore recently. A day on her own might give her some needed rest.

'Well, what I'll do,' I told her, 'is to take the phone off the hook. Then you won't have to get out of bed to answer it every five minutes.' I tidied her bed. 'Have you got everything you need? Can I get you anything from downstairs?'

'I'll be all right,' she replied. 'I just need to rest, put my arm up for a bit. Don't worry. You go. I'll be fine.'

June and I went to Blackpool and had quite a good day, and got back that evening. When we went up to tell Mum all about it her bed was empty.

I looked at the empty bed, and at June. A strange cold fear was taking hold of my insides. 'What on earth has happened?'

'Ring Ann,' said June. 'She might know.'

Ann told us what had happened. She had tried to call Mum on the phone and had found it off the hook, so she had come over to find out what was going on. Mum had got much worse since we had gone, and was by then really sick and in pain. Ann rang John, her husband, who is a doctor. John came immediately and arranged for Mum to be admitted to the hospital in Wigan where he worked.

Two days later the results of her tests came through. Mum had a huge tumor in her neck. It was almost attached to her lung, and it was entwined with the nerves of her shoulder. That was what had caused the pain. Every time she moved her arm her nerves must have shrieked in agony. The biopsy had determined that the growth was malignant. All the painkillers and arthritis treatment had been useless.

The news hardly registered. It was too much to take in. I was angry that Mum's symptoms had not been recognised earlier, but I scarcely took in the fact that Mum was seriously, possibly, terminally, ill. The staff at Wigan gave us the facts straightforwardly. The tumor was inoperable. But the reality only began to sink in a week or so later, when she was transferred to Christies, a big cancer hospital in Manchester.

She was put on a course of anti-cancer drugs there, and was also given radium therapy. She experienced dreadful side-effects. The drugs made her vomit terribly.

The doctors didn't hold out any hope. 'It could take a long time,' they told us. 'We can try to control her pain as much as possible.'

I was numbed with grief and shock. Again, I went to God with my questions. *Please don't let her die*, I sobbed, and gazed at Mum each time I arrived in her ward half-expecting to find her healed. But nothing happened. She was getting worse. The staff at the hospital were very kind to us, and we appreciated how Mum was being looked after. But when they spoke to us you could tell that they were choosing their words carefully, phrasing their words so as not to accidentally offer a hope of recovery.

She was allowed home from Christies and we persuaded her to stay at Ann's house, where John could keep an eye on her progress. Back at home the house was empty and cheerless without her, and the sight of her possessions where they'd been left was almost unbearably painful. June and I had been closer than ever as sisters since I came home. Now we became even closer as we watched Mum's illness taking its course.

We set up a camp bed next to Mum's in Ann's house and we all took turns sleeping beside her. The hospital had given us a supply of pain-killing drugs, but the quantities were strictly controlled, and we were only allowed to give Mum a certain amount. After a while there was nothing you could do for the pain, once that day's ration of drugs had been used up.

I sometimes sat by her bedside reading the Bible to her all night, as she grunted in pain and tried not to shout out as each wave of nausea hit her. *God*, I cried out silently, *why is this happening to us*? In that sickroom I reached out for some sign of God's presence, but only silence came back. Yet I watched in awe as Mum's pain seemed to subside a little as I read to her.

One Sunday at church, one of her friends came up to me. 'I thought your Mum might enjoy this,' he said. He handed me a small flat package.

'Oh, thank you!' I peeped inside the wrapping. It was a cassette of gospel songs by a singer called Len Magee. 'I'll give it to her tonight,' I promised. 'That's very kind of you.' I had reservations, because Mum wasn't really into that kind of thing.

But she loved it. Those songs meant such a lot to her, and I would often arrive at Ann's and find her in the sun lounge listening to them. They were really special to her. I have never been able to listen to them without tears since, because they were so much loved by my Mum in those few weeks.

I knew in my head that God was in control but in my heart I couldn't cope. How can you explain pain? I saw Mum in such distress over those weeks, as the pain-killers wore off and there were no more for her that night. You can't just grit your teeth and say, 'Praise the Lord'. It doesn't always work. It's not that you've lost faith. It's not that your faith has disappeared. It's just that there are times in the Christian life when it's very, very hard and you just have to battle on knowing that God is there even if you can't sense it.

As the days grew into weeks and Mum made no improvement, I slumped into a black spiritual depression. I refused to read my Bible. I refused to pray. I was so angry inside that I often went to bed saying to God, *If you're going to do this to Mum, I'm not even going to speak to you.*

In others' company, I said all the right things. I went to church, to the Thursday meetings and the Preston group meetings. Outwardly, I was the mature Christian undergoing stress. Inside I was being torn apart. It got to the point where I was attacking God in my heart, accusing him of not wanting the best for her – *If you do, why don't you do it?*

But when things were at their blackest I would suddenly find a picture coming into my mind unbidden, a memory of my mother coming into our lounge that Thursday night and telling me that she had given her heart to Jesus. It was as if, through the sadness and the despair, God was saying, *Look, be patient. I am in control. Don't despair. Look what has happened in your Mum's life already.*

July came, and Mum was much worse. Before they knew that I was going to be released, Mum and Ann had booked a holiday at Pontin's Holiday Camp at Blackpool. When I came home they added me to the reservation and the children as well, so it was going to be a real family holiday.

One day in early July, Ann said, 'Of course we'll cancel the holiday.'

We were with Mum, and I agreed but she was adamant. 'You can't cancel it. The children haven't had a holiday for two years. They're looking forward to it so much. It's only a week, after all. You go.'

'Oh, Mum,' I said. 'We can't possibly go. You're ill, and we don't want to leave you.'

'I'll be all right. I'd rather go into hospital. There's no reason for you not to go on that holiday.'

She was so determined, it was making her over-excited. We let the matter drop and later we discussed it together as a family. We decided to follow her wishes, but we didn't want her to go into a hospital. Instead we arranged for her to be admitted into a hospice for the week in Cheadle Hulme near Manchester. It was a lovely place, where the staff were as kind and sympathetic as anybody could wish. They were so understanding.

'Does she know that she is probably going to die from her illness?' Ann and I were asked in a preliminary interview. We explained that we had never spelt it out to her. It just hadn't seemed right.

'We do prefer that she knows,' said the matron gently. But she didn't press the point, and that was good, because we couldn't bring ourselves to break it to Mum. We reasoned that she must have known anyway; she knew about the biopsy, and the pain she was having must have indicated to her how serious her illness was. To spell it out in words seemed like pronouncing the death sentence. So we left it unsaid.

We travelled down from Blackpool twice during that week to see her. She had other visitors too; Herrick went to see her, and so did Jim Hodson, a friend from the Preston prayer group, and several others. Each time I visited Mum I made some excuse to go into the little chapel attached to the hospice and there I raged at God. I shouted my anger and my grief at him and I accused him of cruelty, as all my sorrow at what he was having to do boiled over into rage.

On the Saturday morning we came back home, and went to Auntie Mary's. She opened the door. Her face was very sad.

'The hospice rang. They want you to go there as quickly as you can.'

Mum was conscious, but suffering terribly. The staff had given her massive doses of pain-killer but the pain was defeating them. At intervals a nurse or doctor would appear and administer further drugs. They spoke to us gently and sympathetically. 'She's very poorly,' we were told.

We had arrived there shortly after lunch. We sat at her bedside. After an hour or so I could control myself no longer, and got up quietly. I made my way to the chapel. Pulling open the door, I crept inside. It was empty and curiously cold after the summer afternoon sunlight. I made my way up the aisle and knelt.

There in that deserted chapel I hurled abuse at God. I stormed at him for what was happening. Part of it was grief because my Mum was dying, part selfish fury that such a thing should be happening to me after all I had been through. *I don't want Mum to die. It isn't fair*, I screamed silently. *I don't believe you're even there*, I raged.

It was like lancing an abscess. As the angry, strident thought took shape my rebellion ended. I knew that I simply did not believe the statement I had just made. He *was* there. I knew it was so. After all the sorrows and my Mum's sufferings, I still knew that God had not gone away.

I remained in the chapel a while longer, praying. Then I went back to Mum's ward. We sat there together for several hours. Memories and emotions were filling our minds. We didn't say very much, and there were long silences. The pain made it hard for Mum to say much.

At about eleven o'clock I looked at her and I knew that she was dying. I looked at my sisters. 'Let's pray,' I said suddenly. I prayed aloud. I thanked God for her and for her life.

A little while after that, Mum died.

'I'll tell Sister,' I said. The three of us looked at each other silently. The sadness in Ann and June's faces must have mirrored my own, but in my heart I had an incredible feeling of peace.

I found the Sister. 'My mother's died,' I said.

She looked shocked. 'We didn't expect that,' she said. 'Not now. Your mother could well have lived on for weeks, perhaps months, in that pain. We thought she would have to suffer much longer.'

Mum died in the late evening of July 26, six months to the very day after I stepped from the aeroplane at Heathrow Airport the previous January.

Our neighbours were very kind. Lancashire people are like that. Mum had been much loved in Blackburn, and had many friends. When I was in prison she had as many letters of encouragement as I had, and numerous telephone calls and visitors. Now that she had died we realised more than ever before how many people had been fond of her.

People took the news of her death in different ways. One night not long afterwards I was out for a stroll. It was dark. As I walked past a street lamp, a passer-by saw me and stopped.

'Hello Rita, love.'

I peered at his face in the gloom. I recognised him. He had known our family for years. He had been a regular at the pub my family used to run. We stood talking for a while. He said how sorry he was about Mum, and I told him a little bit about her last few weeks – happy things,

things which I had been cheered up by; things she'd said and done.

He sighed thoughtfully. 'I don't know, love, I don't understand how anybody can say they believe in God after a thing like that.' His troubled voice was genuinely sympathetic. 'When I think of your Dad dying, and then all that's happened to you, and what your Mum suffered while you were in prison . . . and now you're back home she has to go and die. It don't seem right; not right at all.' He sounded angry and upset at the monstrous injustice of it.

I wasn't angry with him. I had felt like that not long before. I knew he meant to be kind. Standing at his side in the pool of yellow light I tried to think what to say to him. I scanned the dark horizon. Above the houses, the moors were indigo smudges against an inky sky. I took a deep breath.

'Well, I do believe in God. I don't understand a lot of what's gone on – but I do believe that he is there and he is real.'

He was taken aback. I hadn't gone out of my way to seek publicity about my new-found faith, and though the newspapers had talked about it quite a bit at the time of my release many local people didn't know that I had become a Christian.

He said goodbye, and I said that I appreciated his sympathy, and that was quite true. Then I went on my way home. I felt sad inside. I remembered my bitter anger at God, the rebellion of the past few weeks. After all the good things God had done for me and for Mum, I'd been capable of turning round and telling him he didn't exist.

But I was also at peace. I had no answers to the questions that Mum's death had raised. Perhaps I never shall have. But looking back, when my rebellion was ended, I could see his hand in everything. He really had been in charge.

Where will you go, I asked myself, *if not to him?* I'd seen both sides, I'd tried my own way and I'd walked in his.

There was no real choice that needed to be made. It really was true. God *was* there, whatever my sadnesses and perplexities.

9: Going On

*In sure and certain hope of the Resurrection
to eternal life, through our Lord Jesus
Christ.*

Book of Common Prayer.

We went through the formalities of bereavement almost
without thinking. John put a note in the 'Deaths' column of
the local newspaper. The next night there was a short
article about Mum, which we appreciated.

The vicar called to discuss Mum's funeral. He was a great
support at a time when we needed help and advice on all
sorts of practical details.

'Herrick knew your Mum best, I think,' he said
thoughtfully. 'He visited her more than I did, so I think it
would be best if he led the service. I'll get him to come
round to see you as soon as possible.'

Herrick was sympathetic and direct. 'Rita, you do believe
that your Mum was a Christian?'

We both knew what he was talking about. I didn't get
involved in theological definitions, I just told him what
Mum had said to me shortly before she died.

'I think she really was a Christian,' said Herrick, when
I'd finished.

'I know she was. And I know where she is now. The Lord
has really comforted me with that,' I said.

In the end Brian and Herrick took the service together, because they both wanted to be involved. Many of the people there were people we'd come to know since I'd arrived back and had been going to the church regularly, but I didn't take notice who was there and who wasn't.

Herrick spoke of the first time he called round to have a cup of tea with Mum; what sort of a person she was; the way she bore up while I was in prison and her courage in her illness. It was a lovely time because both Brian and Herrick not only said wonderful things about Mum but also spoke plainly about the Christian hope, and how Mum had died as a Christian; but it was also a very sad time in all the ways that funerals always are whether you are a Christian or not. I looked at the grief on my sisters' faces, and there was a heavy emptiness in my own heart side by side with the peace which I had felt at the time of her dying and which had not gone away. Mum was no longer with us, and six months had been all too short a time. It would be wrong to say that it was a radiantly happy time for anybody. That's not what the peace of God means.

At the reception afterwards I moved round mechanically, exchanging words with people, shaking hands, being hugged by relatives, but not aware of very much. As a family we survived it all as best we could, and everybody was very kind. We had arranged a meal for visitors, but I couldn't eat a thing. For several days I was unable to eat anything at all. I was already underweight because I had been eating very sparingly since coming home. Now my family became concerned.

'You'll make yourself ill,' they said.

Ill, I thought, *what does that mean? What does anything mean?*

But the emptiness I experienced after Mum died was very different to the black anger I had had during her illness. It was the product of exhaustion and watching somebody through a long illness. We all felt the same, and I think that anybody who has been through a similar experience will know that awful sense of meaninglessness that descends on life just after the person you have cared for for so long finally dies.

It must have been hard for June, as we settled back into domestic life after the funeral. She'd seen Mum upset for so many years by my travelling, and waiting longingly for me to come home. My own attitude wasn't as helpful as it could have been. I found it hard to forget the privileged status I'd had as a foreign prisoner in Lard Yao, and sometimes I think I really irritated her. For her own part, she had been brought up almost as an only child, as Ann and I had left home when she was quite young; so she too felt a bit threatened. I didn't help, being sometimes unable to resist the temptation to criticise when she was doing housework or cooking. I'd forgotten the social graces. In my own mind I was being kind to June, trying to help her to do things more effectively, showing her where she was wrong. In practice I was probably unbearably arrogant.

But we came through that phase, and grew very close to each other again. In a strange way such difficult times can make a relationship stronger than before.

Early in August I telephoned Kathryn Grant in America and told her what had happened. As we talked, I decided that I would try to visit America later that year.

'Give me some time to help sort things out here,' I asked. 'Then I'll come.'

It wasn't a return of the travel bug. That had left me for good. It was a combination of factors – a desire to get away for a break after Mum's illness, a desire to meet my American friends again, and above all an overwhelming curiosity to find out what Prison Fellowship in America was like. I knew bits about it, and I'd read Chuck Colson's books. The Preston group had told me about the work in

England, and how it related to the American situation. But I wanted to go over there to see for myself, because I had such a strong inner conviction that God was going to make it possible for me to work with prisoners and share the gospel with them.

I had a bruising reminder of my own prison record when I was invited into prison in the north of England. I met the Governor at a Christian businessmen's dinner, and he said that he felt a visit from me would be helpful. I was tremendously excited about this, and prayed very hard about it both on my own and at church and with the Preston group. I was advised that the most effective way of gaining admittance was by obtaining a visiting order to see a particular inmate, and this I did. But when I arrived at the prison gates with my form duly completed, I was refused permission to go in.

My first impulse was to argue with the prison officers there and then, and demand to be allowed inside. I contemplated waving my piece of paper at them and insisting on my rights. But I thought better of it, and I had a strong suspicion that my Bangkok prison record lay at the bottom of the whole matter.

So I went home and prayed about it. I was upset, of course, and I just asked the Lord to show me what he wanted me to do. If he did want me to have some sort of a role in caring for prisoners and telling them about him, how could I possibly begin to do so when I'd been told I couldn't even set foot inside the prison?

As I prayed I felt the presence of God in my room, a comforting reality that soothed my distress. Over the next few days and weeks I asked him, *Well, what do you want me to do with my life?* And I began to recognise him saying to me: *What I want is for you to be you, and share what I've done in your life.*

I was dubious about that. To me, speaking in public was

the same as preaching, and I didn't feel that I could possibly be a preacher. But the Lord showed me that the mental picture I had of a preacher was different to somebody simply sharing their own story with a group of people. I began to look forward to whatever the next step was.

In the end I first spoke formally to a public meeting as the result of some astute plotting by Martha Livesey. I was staying with her one weekend, and she took me to various services and meetings.

We arrived at one meeting room which was at the top of a long flight of stairs. As we came in I saw rows of people listening to a lady at the front who was leading the meeting. When she saw us she beamed.

'Praise the Lord,' she said. 'Our speaker has arrived.'

I realised immediately that she was talking about me, not Martha, and I turned tail and ran from the room, heading for the stairs. Martha was after me in seconds and took my arm. 'It'll be all right,' she murmured.

What had happened was that Martha had promised the group beforehand that I would share with them the story of how I became a Christian, but she hadn't told me – because she'd accurately predicted what my reaction would be. I'd never spoken in public from a platform, though of course I'd taken part in lots of informal group discussions and prayer meetings.

Martha knew what she was doing. She didn't throw me in off the deep end and let me fend for myself. She'd arranged for the two of us to be on the platform, she asking questions and me answering. It wasn't long before I found myself telling the congregation the story of what had happened to me in prison, and though I was petrified, I was able to speak clearly and simply.

I had had many invitations to speak since my return, and until then had refused all of them. After the meeting that Martha had 'arranged', I decided that I should start accepting at least a few invitations. I didn't eat for twenty-four hours before the first of them, and was feeling physically sick as I rose to my feet. But as I began to talk a certainty came upon me that I had found what God wanted me to do for him.

Looking back many months afterwards, I realised that the Lord had been telling me that I had to come to terms with speaking in public before I could think of visiting prisons.

I received a large number of invitations to speak, and still more and more arrived. I was reluctant to accept them all, because I saw that it would be possible to become simply a speaker at church meetings, with a ministry of just giving my testimony, being a travelling evangelist. I felt that the Lord was pointing me in a different direction. *This isn't what I have for you. I have another plan.*

But I accepted quite a few of them, and told of my prison experience, and what it was like to receive Christian visitors and know that Christians were praying for me. I urged my hearers to consider the biblical challenge to remember those in prison.

Sometimes I had difficult moments. On one occasion I was given hospitality before speaking at a church, and was confronted at the mealtable by a lady who seemed to have something on her mind.

'Every week, when I was a young woman, I got my pay packet,' she announced.

I waited, munching politely.

'Of course I wasn't saved then, I didn't know the Lord. Well, each week I set aside some money to buy myself something nice. First of all I bought myself a powder compact.'

I nodded approvingly.

'Then the week after that, I bought a lipstick. The next week . . .'

As the catalogue of cosmetics went on I wondered exactly what the point of this story was going to be.

'Then I was saved. It was wonderful. Praise the Lord!'

She told me how it happened, and who had led her to the Lord. 'Then,' she said triumphantly, 'my friend who led me to Christ, and I, we opened my handbag, and we took out all the paint and perfumes – and we threw it down the drain together!'

I was suddenly aware of my own, rather discreet, makeup. I licked my painted lips nervously. 'Huh – are you talking about me? My lipstick?'

She smiled gently at me. 'Well, do you think now, that . . . that makeup is . . .'

I shook my head firmly, and prayed not to lose my temper in front of my host and hostess. 'I'm sorry,' I said, 'but I am sure that for you it is wrong, that it would be a real problem for you to paint your fingernails or use powder. But for me, I don't have a problem with it. Please, leave me alone.'

I was still a young Christian and I had a lot to learn, but it seemed that some Christians were more intent on pointing out what I was doing wrong than on being loving and caring and discussing things in a helpful way. After an article appeared about me in *Today* magazine, with an accompanying photograph of me wearing jeans, I received a letter from one shocked reader quoting Scripture at me and telling me about Jezebel who was thrown to the dogs.

It's true that at that time my clothes were rather more flamboyant and my makeup more noticeable than they have since become. I had much to learn in this area as in many others, and really needed the help of other Christians. But I have to say that sadly, the criticism that some Christians provided me with didn't help me to grow at all. As I considered their comments I felt that many of them had a mental picture of an ideal Christian, to which all young believers should conform. *I don't want to be a stereotype*, I reacted. *I want to be like Jesus.*

Later, I saw exactly the same prejudices standing in the way of some people in the churches accepting prisoners as fellow-believers. Because they wore leather clothes, or because they still had parts of their old life which they were finding it hard to shake off, prisoners often found stiff handshakes and forced smiles the nearest they could get to real fellowship with some Christians.

When I now think back on the setbacks I suffered as a Christian in my early days of being with other believers, it makes me resolve to be extra careful that I do not in my turn hold back some young Christian through my own insensitivity. One such setback it took me days to recover from, was to do with the lady who was organising a big service some way from my home. I was by then fairly well-known as a speaker, and the advertising had drawn in a large congregation. There were posters all round the church which announced the meeting, and other churches in the neighbourhood had been invited. I spoke for three quarters of an hour, and at the end the lady announced that a collection would be taken up. I watched the money piling up; it took quite a while for the plates to go round the hall.

At the end of the meeting I was drinking a cup of tea in a room behind the hall, and the lady organiser was counting up the collection.

'Now, my dear,' she said. 'What are your travel expenses for tonight?'

I told her. She methodically counted out the exact sum in loose change and handed it to me, and put the rest away without further comment.

I was devastated. Not because I wanted money for myself, but because I had hoped that after my talk the money collected would at least in part be given to work among prisoners. Perhaps it was used in that way; possibly, the next day a cheque had been sent as a gift to some prison work. But nobody ever told me, and I never found out what happened to the money generously given on that morning.

Many Christians I met couldn't understand why, with a knowledge of the Thai language, I wasn't going to be a missionary in Thailand. I had to explain that being a missionary was, I believed, a matter of God's call, and I felt God calling me elsewhere.

In fact I couldn't have gone back to Thailand, even had I wanted to. I was *persona non grata* there, and my passport was endorsed. But more than that, I never had wanted to return, which was why I had reacted angrily when, not long after my homecoming, I had heard of a news report about me on television. It was announced that I had 'been refused permission to go back to Thailand'. I was upset to think that people would imagine that, having just left Thailand, I was planning to go back. What would my family think? I had made no such application.

The end of summer saw the return of the national Sunday press. This time they had increased the fee offered by a couple of thousand pounds.

'Have you decided about your story?'

'Story?' I queried, to the journalist at my door.

'Are you interested in doing anything yet? The money's good. I'd think it would come in handy.'

'No, thanks. I don't want to publish.'

The journalist became affable. 'Look, you know we won't be printing anything that hasn't been in print before. It's been over all the papers, you won't be betraying any secrets. You're on Supplementary Benefit, aren't you? Well, then.'

Talking with other Christians later about my refusal to take up the offer – which did indeed come with a great deal of money attached – I had various reactions. Some said I should take the money. It was true, they said; everybody had read the Rita story in the *Daily Mail* and the *Lancashire Evening Telegraph*. Why worry about it being recast? You could give the money to the Lord, use it in his work.

But I pointed out that all the previous press coverage had

been written without my participation, and I have never had the opportunity to tell my own story. I was going to be careful when and how I did that, I said. And did the Lord need money from that source? What was important, after all?

The prospect of capitalising on my release while my friends were still in Lard Yao didn't attract me at all; but if it had, I would have been pulled back to reality by the letter which arrived during August. It was from Linda. She, like Mary her companion, was a black American, very beautiful and extrovert, who had arrived in Lard Yao shortly before I was released. They had joined a prayer group which I and some others had started, and over the time I knew them I had become very fond of them. Both were Christians, and we prayed together about their trials, which were still moving slowly forward, stage by stage, when I left Bangkok.

Linda's letter told me that the day for sentencing had finally come. At the Bangkok courtroom, she and Mary had been sentenced to twenty years each.

I knew how they felt. I too had been given twenty years. But even though they had been expecting the sentence just as I had been expecting mine, it was a crushing blow for them. When I wrote back it was one of the most difficult letters I have ever had to write.

So Summer came to an end, in sorrow for friends in trouble and still with the dull grief of Mum's death in my heart. When Kathryn wrote to me, with a long list of things that Prison Fellowship would like to organise for me to be involved in when I went to the USA, I made up my mind. I wrote to her and asked when she would like me to arrive.

10: Problems Solved

. . . We really rejoice, Rita, and feel that
everything is right for you to come. Now we
are going to join in prayer that the visa will
all work out.

Letter from Kathryn Grant, 25 August
1980

Kathryn's reply was reassuring and calm.

'You need to be in the United States for two months with
all that we have planned,' she explained. She outlined the
results of discussions she had had with Chuck Colson and
Gordon Loux. They had put together quite a programme
which included, 'a period of spiritual study, the dedication
of our new building, and the opportunity to attend one of
our seminars'.

As I read on, I began to be excited by the prospect of
going. It wasn't the travel I was looking forward to. It was
the people I would be meeting. Kathryn's letter continued:

> In October we have ten women prisoners here for
> our seminar. On November 13 there will be a
> meeting and a large gathering of persons who were
> part of the prayer support for you. You will have
> an opportunity to share with them . . .

I was also greatly encouraged by the fact that the staff of Prison Fellowship in the States were praying for me continuously. As I read on I felt the need of those prayers, because the mechanics of getting me into America seemed to be quite complicated:

> In order to enter the United States, because of a prison record, you will have to file a paper with the American Embassy in London called 'Waiver of Ineligibility'. The enclosed letter should be sufficient for you to receive the waiver and your visa.

Now I knew I was finally going to America, I obtained the required form for a visa application. I filled it in without any problems until I came to a section which asked for details of any criminal convictions, drugs offences or prison records. I didn't see any alternative to telling the truth, so I carefully wrote a brief account in the small space provided – my handwriting isn't tiny at the best of times, and there was only space to give the barest outline of events. I sent the form off enclosing the letter that Prison Fellowship had provided, and waited for my visa to arrive.

My application was refused. The letter from the USA Embassy was not unfriendly, but it was absolutely firm. Because of my previous conviction it would not be possible to grant my application.

Lord – what's happening? I prayed. *Please, show me what to do.* It had all seemed so straightforward. Kathryn had even sent me a letter for the Embassy. I had thought there might be some difficulties, but I hadn't dreamed that there would be a flat refusal.

As I prayed, I heard no words and saw no miraculous signs. But inside me there grew a real assurance that God wanted me to go to America for this trip, and that it *would* happen. I also felt that this problem would need hard work on my part. I couldn't just sit back tranquilly and wait for the Lord to work miracles.

I formulated a plan of action. Kathryn had said that ideally I should plan to be in America from mid-September to mid-November. I wrote to her and explained that this would not now be possible. But I also told her that I was sure that this was not the end of the matter. Before, when I'd only just got back to England and then later when Mum was ill, I'd known that it wasn't right to go. Now, I was just as convinced that it *was* right for me to go. All my contact with Prison Fellowship in England, all my telephone calls and letters from America, all my own prayers and thoughts about the future had reinforced my belief, going back to my time in Lard Yao, that somehow my future would be involved with the needs of prisoners. I wanted to go to America because I wanted to find out more about Prison Fellowship and I wanted to spend more time with its full-time workers in the USA. Would it be possible, I said to Kathryn, to come later on – perhaps October, if things were sorted out by then?

As well as writing to Kathryn I telephoned Ross Simpson.

'Read the Embassy letter to me, Rita,' he said.

I read out the letter with its matter-of-fact sentences – regretting that because of the facts I had given it was not possible at this time to grant a visa for entrance into the United States . . . I read on, to the last paragraph, where the writer had added that if I wish to discuss the matter further it would be necessary to attend at the Embassy in person and speak to one of the immigration staff.

'That's what I'm going to do, Ross.' I made up my mind there and then. 'I'll come down on the bus. I'll go and talk to them.'

'Well, all right, Rita. Maybe that's the best thing to do now. Only –'

He hesitated. 'Rita, don't build your hopes up. There's a

lot of red tape involved, and you're not long out of prison.'

'I'll telephone you before I come down,' I promised.

'And I'll see what I can find out in the meantime,' he said.

Before I left Blackburn a telegram arrived from Kathryn. It was brief and emphatic. 'Yes, yes, come.' I rang Ross to say I would be in London the next day. I boarded the bus for London in a very determined state of mind.

London's Victoria coach station was busy with passengers and dozens of vehicles. As the coach pulled in I looked for Ross in the crowds. He was waiting for me as I climbed down. He looked worried.

'Rita, I rang the Embassy this morning. I'm sorry, it's bad news.'

'What did they say?'

'There's no way they're going to give you that visa. Even if you can talk them into giving you that Waiver of Ineligibility, there's a time limit, you have to have been out of prison a certain length of time. I'm afraid you don't qualify, Rita.'

We walked to where his car was parked. I was thinking hard. At the car I squared my shoulders.

'I've got to go, Ross. I've got to go to the Embassy.'

'Sure?'

'I just feel so strongly that I have to go and get the visa.'

Ross smiled. 'All right, Rita. I'll take you round there. Get in.'

Before we said goodbye we prayed together and put the whole problem into the hands of the Lord.

The Embassy in Grosvenor Square was packed with a throng of people. I handed in my letter and explained to the reception officer why I had come. I was instructed to join a long queue of bored-looking people.

I waited for ages, supposing that if I'd got there first thing in the morning, it wouldn't have been so bad, but my coach got in to London at midday and by the time Ross dropped me off at the Embassy the queues were enormous.

In my pocket I had my New Testament, and I squatted on the floor, shifting forward as the queue moved, feeling perfectly at peace as I read. Being in the middle of such a crowd of people could have intimidated me, but didn't. This and all the discouragement I had met with over the visa seemed irrelevant by comparison with the deep sense of peace that I had.

Eventually it was my turn. I was taken into an office where a friendly American official rose from his seat as I entered and shook my hand.

'Miss Nightingale!' he smiled. He scanned the papers in front of him. 'Sit down.' I perched on my chair and looked at him expectantly.

'Now don't worry, Miss Nightingale. I'm familiar with your story. Personally, I myself was a US consul in Turkey. So I believe I can understand something of where you've been. Now, tell me why you want to go to America.'

He was very kind and listened to me carefully as I explained about Prison Fellowship. 'You see, I want to go over there because I think perhaps I can be involved, eventually, in some way.'

As I talked he was scribbling notes on the sheets of paper in front of him. When I'd finished, he smiled at me. 'Fine, I've got the picture. Now I have to make some phone calls.'

He was gone perhaps ten minutes. I sat in the interview room reading my New Testament. It wasn't even enough time to begin worrying. Suddenly he was back.

'Well, Miss Nightingale, you'll have your visa in twenty-four hours.'

I almost hugged him, I was so delighted.

Back at home a letter from Kathryn was waiting for me.

> By now you should have our telegram . . . we want you here so very much, and believe that God works

his own time out. We will plan for your coming as
soon after October 20 as is convenient for
you – then you would return by Christmas to
England.

Kathryn's final paragraph contained wonderful news.

This week Margaret Cole called from
California – she is so in hopes of seeing you. I will
be writing her with your schedule. What a blessing
it was to talk to her . . .

Margaret! With Lucille, she had been so faithful in talking
to me about the Lord when I was in prison. She had visited
me, prayed for me, and rejoiced with me when I became a
Christian. She was only in Bangkok for a part of my time in
prison, but before she left she wrote to the King of
Thailand and offered to serve the remainder of my sentence
for me. The reason that she gave for this astonishing act of
love was that, as she explained to the King, she was nearing
the end of her life and mine had hardly started.

'I believe she has a work to do for God,' she had written,
'among prisoners in many prisons.'

How excited she must have been to know that I was in
touch with Prison Fellowship and was going to America to
see the work at first hand!

And how I praised God, that his timing was indeed
perfect. Not only was I going to America, my visa sorted
out, I was going to see Margaret again.

When within days I also received a letter from Jack and
Gladys Martin, saying that they too would be in America
while I was there – 'We're having a short furlough' – it
seemed as though there was nothing God could possibly do
to make the visit more wonderful.

11: Embarking

We are praying now for wisdom to our loving Father in putting [*your programme*] *together in the way best for you, that he can use for his glory.*

Letter from Kathryn Grant, September 1980

I wrote back to Kathryn exuberantly. I had sorted out my diary, re-arranged what could be re-arranged and cancelled the rest. The travel agent had given me all the details of flights and connections, and I planned to arrive in America on 23 October.

It was over a month before I was due to arrive there, but the time sped by. In a number of ways God confirmed that this was the right thing for me to do next. One problem, for example, was money. Prison Fellowship in America were paying for my travel and hospitality, but I realised that just being in a foreign country again would mean that I would have to have some spending money. (In fact, when I got there, I found that everybody was so kind and generous to me that I hardly needed to spend anything). I'd been receiving Supplementary Benefit for the past few months, but it was only intended to cover essentials, and there wasn't much money to spare. I certainly hadn't any spare cash saved up.

Though I knew this was a difficulty, I didn't worry very much about it. I prayed about it, and the Lord gave me the assurance that it would not be a problem. I didn't advertise the fact that I needed money. Then, shortly before I was due to leave, several gifts of money arrived, totalling about £200. One cheque was for £100; it came in a letter which said, 'We felt that the Lord was telling us to give this money to you.'

In the middle of my preparations I managed to get some other things done. Early in October I went to the Birmingham BBC studios where I recorded a short television broadcast. I had been invited to take part in a series called *The Light of Experience*. Though I welcomed the opportunity to share with hundreds of thousands of people what the Lord had done for me in Lard Yao, I was very nervous. I found it disconcerting to be seated in front of a camera, telling my story to an unseen audience. I'd never done anything like it at all, and my first broadcasting attempt was consequently, despite the help of the producer and studio staff, rather stilted when it was finally released in 1981.

By now I was doing quite a lot of public speaking, and when Tony Ralls, a Prison Fellowship worker in Exeter, invited me to spend a few days in his area I was delighted to accept. Tony had himself been in jail, and since leaving prison he and his wife have developed an extensive ministry with Prison Fellowship.

1980 was turning out a good year for them. With the support of a chain of intercessory prayer-groups – the 'Lydia' groups – they established links between prison chaplains and Prison Fellowship, and links had also been established with Christian businessmen in the locality, the Christian Police Association, and Probation Officers.

In addition, many people in the area were beginning to develop their own ministries in fellowship with Tony and his team; one family, for example, had opened their home to ex-visitors, another had committed themselves to regular prison visiting, and numerous individuals were praying regularly and sacrificially for prisoners by name.

Tony and the members of the fellowship in Exeter and the nearby areas were faithfully putting into practice the biblical command which had inspired Chuck Colson at the very beginning of Prison Fellowship – 'Think constantly of those in prison as if you were prisoners at their side' (Hebrews 13:3).

I was very much looking forward to going down there, and I enjoyed my brief visit very much. I spoke to a group in Exeter and stayed overnight with Tony and his family, returning to Blackburn the next day. Before leaving for Devon I'd visited Martha in Blackpool, so it had been a wonderful week.

The following week Ross had invited me to a conference of Christian Probation Officers in Wales, and I attended it with him the weekend before I was due to leave for America. It was a challenging experience to hear a group of Christians, professionally involved in dealing with problem youngsters, talking together about the relevance of their faith to what they were doing.

Looking back a month or two later I realised that both experiences had been invaluable preludes to my first trip to the United States. The Exeter trip, besides enabling me to see at first hand Prison Fellowship work in the south-west of England, gave me the chance to spend some time with one of the work's pioneers. The conference in Wales showed me that there was more to Christian work among young people than simply preaching the gospel and giving my testimony.

I began to understand something of the importance of a biblical understanding of the whole of life, where the transforming power of Christ reaches into and changes every corner of one's daily existence, not just the 'religious' bits but work, leisure, relationships – everything.

So it was with a sense of having been specifically prepared by the Lord in all sorts of ways that I arrived at London airport to catch the 11.45 flight to Washington.

The flight was comfortable and without incident. I had been to Spain with Mum and June since getting back from Thailand, so it wasn't the first time I had been in a plane since then. But Spain was almost a local journey by comparison with the transatlantic flight; and inevitably, as I gazed at the sun gleaming off the cloudbanks far below the plane, I remembered other long plane journeys.

I remembered the flight to Australia, when I had left home as a teenage bride with my husband to start a new life; the flight from Australia to the Far East less than a year later, my marriage a disaster; the flight back to England for my twenty-first birthday, full of good intentions of settling down, helping my Mum in the pub she ran; the flight back to Australia, part-financed by Mum, both of us aware that my wanderlust had got the better of those good intentions; and then the flight to Hong Kong where I had become a night-club hostess, lived the glamorous good life, acquired a rich and handsome Chinese boy friend and ended up being arrested at Bangkok with three-and-a-half kilos of heroin which had been planted in my baggage.

And then there had been my last long flight, back to England from Kuala Lumpur, having been released from prison in Bangkok by a miraculous royal amnesty. On all the other flights but the last I had been a restless, dissatisfied wanderer, not even knowing what it was I was travelling to find. On the plane back from Kuala Lumpur I was a radiantly happy, joyful Christian, giving thanks to God for his deliverance and all the amazing things that had happened.

Eventually the plane began its preparations for the final airport approach, and it was time to strap ourselves into our seats and adjust our watches to US time. We would arrive in Washington at 10.45 am – an hour before we had left London!

We dropped through the clouds into a bright American morning. Washington lay beneath, stretched out like an architect's model in muted greys and greens. The city disappeared from view behind us as the plane entered its runway approach. As the ground rose to meet us, all I could see for miles around was a thick pine forest. It seemed a very beautiful place to have an airport.

At disembarkation I didn't anticipate any problems. All my papers were in order. I had my visa in my passport, and before the plane landed I checked to make sure that I had all the documents I would need.

I looked again at my disembarkation card, which had given me a temporary headache: filling it out, I had had to think for a while about two questions: one asked what my job was, and the other asked what my income was. I had no job, and I was not coming to America to find one; so after some deliberation I left that section blank. I pondered even longer over the question about income, and in the end I wrote that my income was Social Security in England, but that Prison Fellowship was paying for my trip.

The plane taxied to a stop, the steps were wheeled into place, and I joined the stream of people through the immigration procedures. In the crowd of people at the exit barrier I saw Kathryn, who was waving enthusiastically. I waved back excitedly.

At the passport check a crisply uniformed woman officer glanced at my papers, looked at me, and then looked at my embarkation card again. Her face was suddenly grim.

'How do you intend to live?'

I blinked. 'What do you mean?'

She looked over my shoulder at the long queue behind me. Her manner was abrupt and unfriendly. 'Over there, please.'

She nodded towards a part of the immigration hall where

a number of individual desks were arranged, most of them occupied by people being interviewed. The officer closed her booth and escorted me over to the desk. I glanced across at Kathryn apologetically. She shrugged and made a face. A few bystanders in the queue behind me watched us curiously.

'Now,' demanded the officer. 'How do you propose to live?'

'I don't understand,' I said uneasily.

'Who is supporting you? Is a man supporting you? What are your available means?'

'Well – I've got some money –'

'How much?'

I showed her. She scribbled the amount on a pad, laid the pen down, and waited expectantly for me to proceed. Her face betrayed nothing.

'There's nobody supporting me,' I said. 'I'm here as the guest of Prison Fellowship. Look, it says here.'

I didn't see the point of the questions, and I didn't know why I was being asked them. Later I realised that they were standard 'feelers' designed to trap illegal immigrants and smugglers. But then, I was becoming alarmed. Why on earth were they asking me all these things?

'Into that room, please.' The officer pointed me towards a small interview room. I trailed after her. There were a few other passengers in the room. Nobody was talking to anybody else. As I entered, porters brought my baggage in and dumped it on the table.

It's all happening again. Oh, God, it's all happening again, I cried silently. I began to tremble. Behind me, a male officer entered. I half caught his words. I didn't hear whether it was a greeting, a statement or a question. I just picked up two words – 'arrest' and 'imprisonment'.

He was slightly friendlier than the other officer, but his tone was accusing.

'So when were you in prison, Ma'am?' he asked.

116

'Uh – 1977. I was released in January.'

He seemed extremely surprised, whispered to the woman officer, and left the room. I thought he knew who I was and what my prison record was, and that that was why they were cross-examining me. But watching his reaction I wasn't so sure. Maybe it had been a trick question to find out whether I *had* been in prison.

When he came back he said, 'Well, do you want to tell us about these drugs?'

I was tired and angry by this time. 'What drugs? What are you talking about?'

He took one of my bags and weighed it experimentally in his hand. 'Do you mind if . . .?'

'Look,' I said tightly. 'You can do whatever you want. You can rip the whole lot apart if you want to. I don't care. I'm going to sit over here.'

I stalked across to a bench and sat down, watching them angrily. Then I closed my eyes. *Lord Jesus*, I prayed, *help me. I wasn't expecting this. I don't know what to do.*

I looked up. They appeared to have decided against searching my bags. My briefcase was opened and examined item by item. I was asked to identify each item.

The Prison Fellowship leaflet, in which my story was featured, was taken from my case and put before me.

'What's this?'

'It's just something about Thailand . . .' I replied wearily. Saying 'Thailand' made something snap inside me. I blurted out, 'It just reminds me, you know? I thought there was only one place in the whole *world* where that sort of hassle could happen. But you brought that all back to me. All of it . . .'

I was tearful and upset by now. I was thinking of Kathryn waiting for me at the other end of the arrivals hall. She would have been waiting for over half an hour by now. 'Look,' I pleaded, 'there's someone waiting for me outside. Can you send a message to say I'm delayed?'

'Sooner we're through, sooner you're with your friend, Ma'am.' The reply was firm but slightly less unfriendly. They finally finished going through my briefcase.

'How long is your visa for?'

'Two months.'

'Well, we'll just have to stamp it, Ma'am.'

The words 'Not to exceed two months' were added to my hard-won visa.

'OK Ma'am, you can go now.'

Within minutes I was being hugged by Kathryn and being taken out of the airport, away from the officials, the questions and the panic.

Talking about it all afterwards, my hosts thought that the problem was not the fact that I had a prison record, but that by filling in the disembarkation card as I had, I had aroused the officials' suspicions. They had held me back to see whether my incomplete replies meant that I was attempting to enter the country illegally, and were probably quite taken aback to find out what my history actually was.

I had assumed that because my visa had been granted and my name was presumably on a computer somewhere, it was all sorted out. I hadn't realised that getting a visa and actually entering the country are two quite different things.

Looking back, I felt that it could have been worse. After all, the last time I had had an experience like that in an airport, I had gone from the airport into police custody. Relaxing with my new American friends, I began to put the incident behind me.

'Wow, though,' I said to Chuck Colson later, 'they didn't half give me a hard time.'

He grinned at me sympathetically. 'Rita, I still get that. They do that to me even if I'm just going to Canada. It's having a prison record, you see.'

Somehow that made me feel a lot better.

12: Washington, DC

My greatest joy was a week spent early in my visit with a group of ten women released through Prison Fellowship from their various institutions to complete an intensive two-week discipleship course in Washington, DC.

Prison Christian Fellowship (UK),
Regional and Development News, Spring
1981

With Kathryn Grant at the airport was Vivien Nielson, with whom I was to stay. I was given a wonderful welcome. I quickly forgot the worries in the immigration offices, and was soon relaxing in Vivien's beautiful home.

I knew very little about Prison Fellowship, though I had corresponded with Kathryn and the others in America, and seen first-hand the work that was beginning in Britain. Any worries that I might have had about my inexperience were quickly forgotten – I had no time to think about it!

The first function which I was to attend was already in progress when I arrived in Washington. The 'Prison Fellowship Twenty-Sixth Graduating Class' had commenced on 19 October and was due to end on November 1. This was the seminar which Kathryn had told me of in her letters, and which was to be one of the main events of my visit.

'We have ten women and girls,' explained Kathryn over dinner, 'all of whom have been released from prison for the period of the seminar. They are staying in the home of a Prison Fellowship associate who has loaned the house for this fortnight.' She riffled through a sheaf of papers. 'Look – this is the schedule for the seminar.'

I took the paper and shook my head in disbelief. 'You mean they're allowed out of prison – just like that? That's incredible!'

Kathryn nodded 'There are chaperons with them, but really the prisoners are on ten days parole leave.'

'I can't imagine that happening in England,' I said impulsively. 'It's a wonderful idea.'

'We're praying it will happen in England, one day – soon,' said Vivien. 'You've no idea how great it is, to hear how they share all that God is doing in their prisons. And it's a time of really intensive Christian training for them.'

I looked at the timetable in front of me. It certainly was packed. 'Where is Ligonier Valley?' I asked.

'It's a Christian study centre,' explained Kathryn. 'The first week, the women go there for a period of residential study. Now they're back in Washington, and you'll be meeting them very soon!'

We talked for a while about the seminar, and chatted about all the things that had happened since my release. I was enjoying the evening tremendously, but was having difficulty keeping my eyes open. While it was still quite early, Vivien smiled at me apologetically.

'There'll be lots of time to talk, Rita. We're so glad you're here at last. But now you should get some sleep. Don't feel you have to be up early tomorrow!'

One of the attractive things about the seminar programme was the very thorough hospitality programme which Prison Fellowship had arranged for the seminar participants. A 'family sponsorship' scheme made sure that each of the women was entertained in somebody's home several times during the fortnight. On the first Saturday, two days after my arrival, Vivien entertained one of the girls from the seminar for lunch and supper. It was a memorable day. I really liked Alie, I enjoyed being with Vivien, and we went to the Air and Space Museum in Washington, which was well worth seeing – I've always been an enthusiastic sightseer when abroad.

Alie was very fashionably dressed, and it was difficult to imagine her in prison, much less doing prison chores and being part of that grey, shapeless prison population. She was attractive, smart and fun to be with.

The next day I went to church with my hosts, and afterwards there was a buffet reception for the seminar participants. It was quite crowded and I didn't identify who they were until somebody pointed them out to me. I suppose I was expecting them to look alike in some way, to be a recognisable group; to be wearing identical clothes or identical expressions. But it was quite different. The prisoners looked gorgeous – beautiful clothes, smart high-heeled shoes, very well made up. Most of them were black. They were radiant.

The other amazing thing about the prisoners, besides their stunning looks, was their singing. During the time I got to know them they sang a great deal, and there was no mistaking them as a group then. I never heard singing like it.

We all – Prison Fellowship staff, associates, seminar participants and others involved – stood up one by one and introduced ourselves. We said who we were and where we'd come from. When it came to my turn I got up hesitantly and said, 'My name's Rita Nightingale, I only just arrived in Washington, I'm spending two months with Prison Fellowship staff here.' I was feeling very new and rather overawed by the situation, not least by the attractive, radiant women and girls who were the focus of the whole event. We all chatted afterwards; people were welcoming and interested – many of them said they had prayed for me while I was in prison – but I was awkward and shy, and had to rack my brains for things to say. Chuck Colson made his way through the throng of people and welcomed me. It was lovely to see him again. As the evening progressed, I began to feel more at home and to enjoy the warmth of hospitality surrounding me.

I was still feeling overawed the night before I was due to give my first formal talk to the group. A series of different speakers each talking about something they were involved in or expert in was a major feature of the seminar, and I was to speak about my experiences in Hong Kong and Lard Yao.

That night I lay in bed feeling terrible fear. What could I possibly have to say to these smart, amusing women, with their vibrant personalities, laughter and marvellous singing voices? I'd held my own with Alie with no problems, but that had been different. Alie was just one person, and at Vivien's house there had been more of 'us' than of her. But tomorrow I was to talk to the whole group. *I should never have come*, I thought wretchedly. I wasn't a prisoner any more. I'd begun to forget all sorts of things. Would I even be able to relate to prisoners?

I prayed about it, telling the Lord how frightened I was, and began to feel more at peace. Inside me I had an assurance that it would be all right, that it wouldn't be a fiasco.

Next morning I still had that feeling of peace deep inside me, but I was still nervous as I thought about the meeting. Kathryn drove me to Prison Fellowship headquarters, where the session was to be held. I was shown into a conference room, where the women and girls were sitting in an informal semicircle. My doubts began to return. Did I really have anything in common, anything worth communicating, to this group? I felt a few moments of total insecurity and self-doubt. Then into my mind came the thought, unprompted, *Of course you have something to share. They are prisoners. So were you.*

We went to the front of the room. Kathryn introduced me to the group. Then she smiled at me and nodded. I rose to my feet shakily. The circle of women gazed at me expectantly. There was no clue in their faces as to what they might be thinking about me.

'Hello,' I said. The circle of faces smiled back at me. I cleared my throat and started again. 'Hello. I just want to share with you today what the Lord did for me in my life while I was in prison . . .'

As I spoke I began to relax. My doubts left me. After all, I had spoken to small groups, in fellowships and churches. I'd given my testimony quite a few times. In a way I had become well-practised in summarising my story and testifying to what the Lord had done in my life.

'I thought I was the smart one,' I told the group. 'I thought I knew it all. But I was the mug.'

It was the same story I had told many times already, in small prayer groups in Lancashire, in churches wider afield, seated under the hot studio lights in front of the cameras, recording *The Light of Experience* for British television.

But this time it was different.

As I spoke on, I felt myself gripped by what I was saying. I was aware of someone guiding my mind and my voice, telling me what to remember and how to say it. I wasn't just narrating the story, I was *sharing* it in a way I had never done before. I poured out the story both of my spiritual crises and becoming a Christian, and of what I had been through in prison as a woman. 'I swore, I screamed, I was bitter and angry,' I recalled, and saw answering nods of recognition as I said it.

Suddenly there was nothing I wanted to hold back from

these women. I wanted to share with them everything that the Holy Spirit brought to my mind. I told them about my ambitiousness, my restless search for happiness that had taken me halfway round the world, my fascination for the glamour and night life of Hong Kong which had led me step by step further and further into trouble. And I shared my experiences in Lard Yao prison. But it wasn't particularly easy to speak, because I was finding it extremely emotional. Part of the time, my throat tensed as if I were about to burst into tears, and I had to struggle to finish.

I finished, pulled myself together and looked round at the women and girls.

Over half of them were in tears. I stood there, breathless, with an extraordinary sense of individual love for each person in that room. There was silence for about a minute. I wasn't sure what to do.

Then one of the women, a big, very beautiful black girl in her twenties, got up and came over to me, tears streaming down her face. She put her arms round me and gripped me tightly.

'I know,' she said; 'Oh, I *know* . . .'

Afterwards we all hugged each other, and wept and laughed together for what seemed a long time. There was such an overpowering feeling of fellowship that it seemed impossible that I had ever felt shy of these people.

It was the first time that I'd had contact with prisoners since I had left Lard Yao.

From the point of view of my American visit as a whole, that session was a very small part of the whole thing, and it happened right at the beginning. But for me personally it would be no exaggeration to say that it was a turning point in my life. I now *knew*, without a shadow of doubt, that I wanted to work with prisoners.

It was such a terrible situation to which they were soon to

be returning. I knew something of American prisons from reading Chuck Colson's books and talking with various people. I had my own experiences of prison. I knew the daily ridicule they would receive from their fellow inmates, the cynicism and hostility, the accusations of false piety and of being 'wardens' pets'. So I could see how important it was that they should have had this special time of fellowship, study and training in discipleship.

But at the same time I could see how important it was for them to be reminded and encouraged in their role as ambassadors of Jesus in their prisons. Hundreds of prisoners would watch these women as they lived their daily lives, and by their example would see the power and the grace of God. We could never reach those hundreds in the normal ways open to us. But they could – and would – be in contact with them, sometimes for years.

God opened my eyes that week to the limitless power of a ministry among prisoners, if that ministry is truly consecrated to him. I became gripped with the excitement of the vision of Prison Fellowship, which had begun out of the ruins of a disgraced Presidential Counsel's life, and was now bringing hope and new life to hundreds. I wanted to be part of it. I wanted to commit my life to it, for as long as God wanted me to be involved.

For the week of the seminar I was scheduled to stay in the home of Gordon and Beth Loux, of the Prison Fellowship staff. But when it was time for me to move there from Vivien's home, I plucked up my courage to suggest a change in the arranged plan. I asked to be allowed to move into the house where the prisoners and their chaperons were staying. I wanted to spend as much time as possible with them. Arrangements were made for me to do this.

During that week I was with them wherever they went and whatever they were doing. It was an exhilarating time. They had been released from prison to attend the seminar,

125

so there was all the excitement and relaxation of a holiday – I could well identify with that, because I could imagine what it would have meant to me to be let out of Lard Yao for a fortnight to live in a lovely home in suburban Washington! But there was also the thrill of fellowship in such very special circumstances – for some of the girls it was the first time they had ever met with other Christians outside prison. There was a sense that every moment of every day was precious, because the time was so short.

On the last Sunday the seminar came to an end with a Dedication Service at Falls Church in Washington. I was invited to speak at it. I will never forget that service, because it drew together so many of the new and exciting things I had been experiencing. In the morning I had attended another service where Fred Rhodes had been preaching. He was the person whom Chuck Colson, five years earlier, had invited to be his personal administrator when, after his release from prison, his paperwork was beginning to increase beyond one man's ability to handle. Invitations to speak and letters on many different topics were arriving at the Colson household from all sorts of places, and to add to the problem Chuck was trying at that time to finish writing *Born Again*, his account of his Watergate involvement and surrender to Jesus Christ. Fred Rhodes had restored order to Chuck's desk and brought a wealth of varied and distinguished experience to bear on his administrative problems. He had been Chuck's first colleague in the prison ministry and was deeply involved in the founding of Prison Fellowship.

As I listened to him that morning it was good to be able to fit a face to the name I had come to know well. It was to Fred Rhodes that Jack and Gladys Martin had written when I was in Lard Yao, and he had circulated my request for prayer throughout the United States and in other countries. In fact he had been in Bangkok shortly before my

126

release, and had applied to visit me but had been refused.

The Dedication Service in the afternoon was led by a number of those who had led sessions in the seminar or had been involved in its organisation. The members of the seminar were introduced one by one and presented with certificates, stating that they had attended and completed the programme. Then they took turns to speak about what the seminar had meant to them. Woman after woman testified to the deepening of their faith, a renewed commitment to Jesus. They spoke movingly of where they had come from and what it was like to be a Christian in prison; and they talked about going back there, and what their hopes and fears were. It was a sober time, but also an inspiring one.

When it was my turn to speak, Kathryn introduced me to the large congregation. When I rose to face them I was a little nervous, but I was no longer talking to strangers. Sitting in front of me were the women and girls I had come to know and love in such a special way in one short week.

13: Learning

*I've had a pretty full schedule, but I've been
receiving so much from the Christians around
me.*

Letter to the congregation of St. Andrew's,
Blackburn: published in the December
1980 parish magazine.

That night I made my belated arrival at the home of
Gordon and Beth Loux. It was a lovely family home, and
Gordon and Beth welcomed me warmly. Gordon controlled
the day-to-day operation of the Washington office. I stayed
with them for a week, much of which I spent in the office
observing what was going on and the various activities of
the Fellowship.

Until then I had been unclear about how the various parts
of Prison Fellowship fitted together, and how the prayer
group in Preston and Sylvia Mary in London fitted into the
overall situation. Now I learned that there were two linked
organisations: Prison Fellowship USA was the movement
originally spearheaded by Chuck Colson as the result of
God's guidance to him in prison; and Prison Fellowship
International brought together people and fellowships all
over the world, and had come into being largely because of
the many people around the world who had read Chuck's

books and wanted to be involved. Chuck Colson was Chairman of the International and the USA Fellowships; Gordon Loux was President and Kathryn Grant Vice-President of Prison Fellowship International.

The organisation in England – Prison Christian Fellowship – was part of the Prison International Fellowship, by whom I had been invited to America. Sylvia Mary Alison was its Chairman, and the English representative on the International Council.

It sounds complicated, but it seemed to work well. The offices of Prison Fellowship USA and Prison Fellowship International were at that time in the same building, so I had an excellent opportunity to gain an overview of what was happening. I was taken aback to discover what a huge ministry Prison Fellowship, in all its aspects, had. Seminars were continually taking place, many of them inside prisons. Each entailed an enormous amount of paperwork – initial negotiations with prison authorities, whether requesting permission for individuals to be allowed 'furlough' to attend an out-of-prison seminar, or for an in-prison seminar to be held and prisoners to be allowed to attend. In some cases there was considerable resistance, in others Prison Fellowship was well-known and its visits encouraged. Each seminar was carefully planned and prayed over.

Then there was follow-up – the Fellowship maintained large files of prisoners and ex-prisoners with whom they were in touch. Sometimes a correspondent would need counselling, sometimes there were practical problems in which it was possible to lend a helping hand. Occasionally an ex-prisoner could be put in touch with a Christian employer prepared to offer a job – just as in Britain, a prison record makes it virtually impossible to get a good job in America, but the Fellowship, which is based on trust between Christians, has made it possible for many ex-prisoners to begin a new life.

Besides the needs of the prisoners the work among the

supporters and prayer-partners was a major part of the daily activities. The quarterly newsletter, *Jubilee* (the first issue of which after my release had featured my story, so that the hundreds in America who had prayed for me could know how my release had happened), gave an indication of the numbers of people involved.

There were Prison Fellowship organisations, I discovered, in Australia, Canada, England and New Zealand as well as America. Most operated like the English organisation, centering the work on small groups of praying Christians who worked and prayed to arouse the Christian community in their locality to the needs of prisoners. Groups like these had prayed for me when I was a prisoner, in 'prayer chains' in Australia and America.

Much of my time in the office was spent writing letters to prisoners all over the world, many of whom had written to Prison Fellowship International since my release expressing their good wishes and asking to be put in contact with me.

It was a long time since I'd worked in an office, and I enjoyed the friendliness. It wasn't a grand suite designed to impress the visitor with the wealth and prestige of the owner. It was efficient and pleasant, and it looked out to green fields in which horses grazed. It had one striking feature. The room had originally been divided by a system of screens into one or two smaller offices. You could see how, as the operation had grown in size, further subdivisions had taken place, and yet more. At the time I saw it, the Prison Fellowship International office was composed of the smallest cubicles I'd ever seen. Everybody tolerated the situation with great good humour, and it was a dramatic visible sign that God was blessing the work and making it grow!

After my week in the office, November was a whirlwind of visits and events. For the next fortnight I travelled. From 2nd-7th November I was in California, where I had a hectic programme, mainly speaking to churches. It was hard work but I was buoyed up the whole time by the warmth of the welcome I received from everybody I spoke to, many of whom had prayed for me while I was in prison.

When I returned to Washington I worked in the office again, and amongst the letters I wrote was one to my home church, St. Andrews. I listed the schedule I had for the remainder of my visit, and asked for prayer as I undertook the various commitments.

> I'd appreciate your prayers very much. God is leading me into a deeper understanding and commitment. I may not like some aspects of it, but I praise him that he is using me. Pray that I will have the courage of my convictions.

My schedule was, I reported, as follows:

14-20	November:	The Study Centre for Discipleship Training.
21-24	November:	Denver, Colorado; fellowship and sharing with various churches.
1-3	December:	Visiting prison in West Virginia. Meeting some of the women I met at the Washington Seminar and speaking in the prison chapel.
4	December:	Speaking at a church in Washington.
7	December:	Speaking at a very large church in Virginia.
10-12	December:	In New York, seeing publishers for a book. Special prayer for me.
21	December:	Speak at a women's luncheon.
23	December:	Fly home.

In between these dates I was usually in the office, writing

letters and getting to know more and more about the work of the Fellowship.

The 'Study Centre for Discipleship Training' was the Ligonier Valley Study Centre, where the women from the seminar had been for the week before I met them in Washington. Now it was my turn to go, for Prison Fellowship had arranged for me to study there for a week.

Ligonier is a beautiful brick-and-timber house in a property in the Laurel Highlands near Pittsburgh. A variety of courses of study are offered, and I had been registered for the general study programme.

The other students were on long courses, and I was registered for just one week. It would have been easy to treat it as a holiday – the atmosphere was very friendly, I enjoyed meeting the other students, and the countryside around was very tempting. But before very long I was enthralled by what was going on.

It wasn't just that it was a lovely place to be, that the people were very nice, and that it was in many ways more of a retreat than a training session. I think I could have spent the week relaxing and doing nothing if I had wanted to. But I sat in on two lectures and listened to a number of taped talks.

It was a revelation. I'd never heard concentrated biblical teaching before; subjects like the holiness of God were opened up in a way that thrilled me, and I drank it all in. I sat up half the night in the audio laboratory with headphones over my ears, and I was struck dumb by it all; sometimes I was in tears as I listened. I was seeing things I'd never seen before – it was so real and so simple at the same time. As I listened to 'RC' (as R. C. Sproul is called by all his students), I began to understand what the apostle Paul meant when he talked about 'the unsearchable riches of Christ'. You could study things like that for a lifetime and barely scratch the surface, yet under a hospital hut in a

Bangkok prison I had understood all I needed to know that God loved me and that I belonged to him. As I became gripped by the excitement of it, I hungered to know more and more. I didn't see how any Christian could fail to be excited by finding out what a great God we have. The word 'theology' is such a dull label for what it represents!

Ligonier marked the beginning of a desire to study, and was a very special time when I seemed to be able to absorb all sorts of teaching that I'd previously not been ready for. It was a privileged period. While the excitement hasn't faded since then it hasn't always been possible to keep going at the same pace, and while there have been times when I've been gripped by study and the 'deep' things of the Christian faith, there have been many more when I've just read my Bible and prayed and been content to feed on the things I've already learned. The picture of feeding is quite helpful, in fact; after you've eaten a large and satisfying meal you don't go out and eat another immediately!

But learning wasn't an intellectual exercise that served just to stimulate my mind. I discovered very quickly that when you learn any real truth about the Lord, your life changes because of it. One night I was listening to a tape by somebody who had been a prisoner of war in Korea. It was a tape on the subject of forgiveness – something I thought I knew a bit about, after my experiences in Lard Yao. But I was jolted awake by what the man said.

Imprisonment had confused his mind, he explained. He had seen himself and his companions acting irrationally and completely out of character. 'Prison does that to you', he went on. 'It messes up your mind. We're not all of us in prison in the way I was,' he added. 'But in a sense we are. And because we've all had our minds messed up by being imprisoned in this fallen world, we've got to change. We've got to see things differently.'

I remembered my own feelings as I had sat under the hospital hut in prison, just after my own meeting with God, looking out across the dusty yard at the anonymous figures in the distance. *The whole world's in prison,* I had realised, *and I've just been shown the way out.* I really understood what the man on the tape was saying. I remembered my painful exercises in forgiveness, as I had struggled, with the help of my few Christian friends who had access to the prison, to learn to forgive. It had been a bruising, daily process, laying aside real and imaginary hurts and coming to Jesus again and again seeking his help in learning to love the people I had hated.

The Lord brought me out of prison with a mind that had been changed, but the change was not complete; now in Ligonier I realised that I still had bitterness in my heart, a bitterness largely directed at Hannah; Hannah, the prisoner who had taken me under her wing when I arrived in Lard Yao and with whom I had had a stormy friendship which had eventually shrivelled into frigid antagonism. When I had left prison I'd found it impossible to say goodbye to her, my emotions were so mixed up. I'd taken refuge in the fact that I was leaving and she wasn't, so I could forget her. And I had, but now I found myself remembering her again; the good times, the bad times, the laughs, the arguments. *She can't hurt me any more,* I reflected. *When she did hurt me, it was prison that made her like that.*

I wrote a long letter to Hannah. 'I'm sorry,' I wrote. 'I know you didn't like me, for many reasons; but I know that you did like me in some ways as well. And I know that that place did things to both of us . . .' I apologised for not having written to her before. 'And we left on such a bad note,' I added. 'But I hope we can somehow put that all behind us. I hope you'll feel able to write to me.'

She replied immediately, and we began exchanging letters every month. And that was one very practical working-out in my life of the things that the Lord was teaching me. Whoever said that doctrine and Bible Study are boring!

For the rest of my time in America I travelled a good deal, speaking in public and seeing many aspects of Prison Fellowship at first hand.

One disappointment was that it seemed to be impossible to fit in a visit to Jack and Gladys Martin. They were on furlough in Louisiana. Early on in my visit I discussed with Kathryn how I might possibly visit them.

But America is a large country. After looking at the distances involved we both regretfully came to the conclusion that it wouldn't be possible to fit such a trip into my already crowded schedule. The cost would be so high that it wouldn't be right to take it from Fellowship funds – most of which had been donated by people specifically intending their gift to be used in work among prisoners.

It was a blow, but I completely understood that it wasn't possible. I know that Kathryn tried several ways of solving the problem and contacted a number of people who might have been able to help, but nothing worked out. She was as disappointed as I was, because she knew how much I would have loved to have seen them again.

We prayed about it several times, asking the Lord whether there might be some way in which I could go to Louisiana after all. Then we left it in his hands.

'We've allocated you eight-and-a-half minutes,' said the efficient organiser. I swallowed apprehensively, and clutched my piece of paper.

Kathryn and I were at a huge Baptist convention in Washington. She had warned me in advance that I would be speaking for that length of time, and I'd sat up late and worked out what I was going to say and how best to fit it into the time given me. Then I'd carefully written it all out in the form of notes.

When it was my turn to speak I stood at the lectern and gazed at hundreds and hundreds of people in rows that seemed to stretch away into the distance. I froze. *Lord, I can't do it,* I pleaded. My tongue seemed like a block of wood; I couldn't open my mouth.

Then as if by instinct I dropped the piece of paper with my notes on it. As it fluttered to the floor I found I could open my mouth again. I spoke for eight-and-a-half minutes and said what I wanted to say.

I learned a valuable lesson from that experience – apart from the fact that it was the only time I ever tried to speak from notes (though I know others find it helpful to do so, I just can't do it). The Lord taught me that any gift I might have as a speaker and communicator was given to me by him. It was sobering to discover that speaking in public wasn't something that I could do in my own strength, but it was encouraging too. God was in control, and I could trust him.

He had more for me in that convention, too. One of the main speakers was a man who worked at the Baptist Radio headquarters in Texas. He introduced himself to me and gave me an exciting invitation. 'Would you come down to Dallas to do some radio work for us? Of course we'll pay all your expenses.'

Jack and Gladys! I thought, and immediately turned to Kathryn, my eyes sparkling. 'Kathryn – is that anywhere near Louisiana?'

'Not far away!' she smiled.

I only had to be in Dallas for one day and night, and then I made the short journey to Louisiana.

I spent two days with Jack and Gladys. We walked endlessly, laughed a lot and wept a little and thanked the Lord together for the way in which he had made it possible for us to be together for that time.

Meeting Margaret Cole was easier. I had special links with her church in Los Angeles. The minister Wilbur Wacker and his wife Shirley had been in Bangkok during my imprisonment and had visited me in Lard Yao. So I was special to them as they were to me, and the church had been praying for me ever since. When they knew I was coming to America, the minister had contacted Prison Fellowship and arranged for me to visit the church.

I arrived at Los Angeles airport, and Margaret met me. I shrieked with delight when I saw her and gave her an enormous hug. She was wearing a gorgeous flamboyant pink dress, and her face was wreathed in smiles.

She led me to a huge car, talking enthusiastically, and we threaded our way through the Los Angeles traffic. I gasped involuntarily several times as it seemed that she would never be able to steer the vehicle between the elusive gaps in the unending flow of cars and trucks, but she wove in and out expertly, chatting nonchalantly as she drove.

We talked for hours, making up for all the frustration there had been in Bangkok when we had only had brief, noisy visiting sessions in which to talk and the all-too-short farewell party on my last day in Thailand. When we had caught up with each other's news, she told me all about her ministry in America and I told her what I was doing in Prison Christian Fellowship.

When later I spoke at her church I felt completely at home. I knew that I was speaking to people who had prayed for me a long time. It was a joy to be with them and to be able to tell them, as I was able to tell so many during my American visit, what it had meant to know that at every hour of the day and night somebody, somewhere in the world, was praying for me, that I would be released, and that until that day the Lord would be close to me and give me peace.

Of all the things I said from platforms in America, that was the thing I said most often. I wanted to thank people, to remind and encourage them, to tell them that praying for prisoners does make a difference.

In my travels and in Washington, I got to know many of the Prison Fellowship staff well. One with whom I established a special friendship was Ferne Sanford, Resource Officer of Prison Fellowship International. I was scheduled to stay with her after my time with Beth and Gordon Loux. She had been involved in Christian work in Africa, and was now living in a 'hospitality house' attached to one of the churches. We struck up an immediate friendship, and when I left we said goodbye with real sadness, and a promise from Ferne to visit me when she came to England later in the year. She was somebody very special whom the Lord provided for me at that time. I was able to relax with her, have fun and unwind after the hectic round of each day's new experiences.

There was much to see. I saw small groups which had only just been formed, in areas where Prison Fellowship was just beginning its work. I spoke to established groups and church congregations, school classes and groups meeting in people's homes. Everywhere I went I was made welcome.

As I came to the end of my visit I reflected on what I had learned and I certainly had a lot to think about. Nothing had prepared me, for instance, for the standard of living enjoyed by many Americans. I had met more wealthy Christians during my stay than I had thought existed, and for a time it bothered me. But as I got to know them I found most of them incredibly generous. Many of them shared their prosperity freely, making no distinctions about whom they helped and why. I was given many lovely presents, including a wardrobe of clothes and a splendid leather wallet stuffed with money. But I also saw many examples of generosity where the people who benefited weren't people like myself on a speaking tour. I know what the Bible means when it says that riches cause many problems – sometimes I think they cause more problems than they cure! – but I also know that I experienced the presence of the Holy Spirit in wealthy Christian homes in America as clearly as I have felt his presence in prison cells and ordinary homes in England.

But apart from the culture-shock, I had been revitalised. 'I was losing touch,' I wrote to my friends at St. Andrew's. 'But God showed me a "mountain top", a vision of what is possible in England.'

For indeed my thoughts were turning back to England, where I had so many friends who were working and praying to build a similar ministry among prisoners to that which I had seen in Washington and in my other travels.

America had been a whole new world, full of exciting and unimagined experiences. Now I was looking forward to going home. I was beginning to feel that this was the work I was meant to do. Somehow, in England, I knew that there would be an opportunity to commit myself to it.

14: Starting Work

We are not promised guidance far ahead, nor
are we assured that we shall always know
how God is going to work; but we are
promised that, as and when we need to make
decisions, God will overrule and guide.

Oliver Barclay, *Guidance* (1966),
chapter 1

I arrived back in England very early on the morning of
Christmas Eve. Ross Simpson met me at Heathrow
Airport, before I flew on to Manchester and home. I came
in out of the murky cold and dark into the bright lights of
the reception lounge and there he was, looking tall and
familiar. He hugged me and manoeuvred me through the
crowds thronging the complex. We found a coffee bar and
talked for ages. I had lots to tell him. Ross listened carefully
and sympathetically, punctuating my narrative with 'Praise
the Lord!' whenever I stopped for breath. It was one of
Ross' favourite expressions, but always sounded fresh and
meaningful when he used it. It certainly echoed my feelings
then.

It was quite a time before I slowed down and sipped my
coffee, by then almost cold. 'It was wonderful, Ross. I've
come back with such a vision for prisoners. It's changed my
life.'

Ross smiled at me thoughtfully.

'I'm so glad you had a good trip, Rita. Praise the Lord. We were praying for you all the time.' He hesitated. 'Rita, we've been thinking and praying for some time about this, and now we feel that the Lord is definitely leading us to invite you to work with us full-time. We'd like you to consider becoming a member of Prison Christian Fellowship staff here in Britain.'

I was speechless. It was a completely unexpected invitation. While in America I'd felt God telling me very directly that I was somehow to work with prisoners, but I hadn't yet worked out how I was going to go about it.

Ross smiled at my excitement. 'You must realise, Rita, we couldn't pay you a large salary. Not what you'd probably be able to get somewhere else. Prison Christian Fellowship isn't a rich organisation. We would pay you more of a retainer.'

I found my voice again. 'I don't think that would be a problem . . .'.

'We do feel very strongly that you should be a part of what God is doing in the Fellowship,' he added. 'We feel that it's important. Will you pray about it?'

'Oh, yes, I'll certainly pray about it . . .' I promised, my head whirling. Ross beamed.

'Pray about it and have a good think about what it would mean, the changes you'd have to cope with. You know how we work. You'd be travelling a lot, speaking – let us know when you've decided.'

I said I would. 'Praise the Lord!' said Ross. But I think I had already made up my mind. I knew an answer to prayer when I saw one.

I went home to Blackburn and Christmas with June and Ann. I gave them the presents I'd bought for them in America and told them all about my trip, and we had a lovely Christmas, even though there was sadness as well because it was our first Christmas without Mum. I enjoyed being in church at Christmas time. For the first time I was celebrating the birth of somebody I knew personally, in a congregation of his friends.

I told my family a little of what Ross had said at the airport, but I didn't go into details. For most of the holiday I hugged the secret to myself, and whenever I could I talked to God about it, half-afraid that I would suddenly receive a dramatic assurance that this was not the way he wanted me to go. I was open to whatever he wanted me to do. But I did hope that working with Prison Fellowship was what he wanted!

But as I prayed and read my Bible, the conviction grew stronger and stronger in my heart that God had clearly shown me exactly what his plan for my next step was. Looking back I remembered my growing concern in Lard Yao, not just for the prisoners there, but for prisoners all over the world. How thrilled I had been when I had first found out about Prison Fellowship, when Kathryn Grant had visited me in prison and left me Chuck Colson's book!

I remembered the letters that had awaited me when I arrived home, Chuck's telegram, the letter from Sylvia Mary, the increasing opportunities to be involved in local activities of the Fellowship. At the time it had sometimes seemed a random sequence of events. But looking back, it was as if a straight line connected my arrival at Lard Yao, a confused and bitter prisoner, and the conversation I had had with Ross at London Airport on Christmas Eve four years later.

So, shortly after Christmas, I found myself back in London, sitting with Ross, John Harris and Sylvia Mary, at Sylvia Mary's house.

'As Ross has explained to you, Rita, we will pay you a retainer.' Sylvia carefully explained the terms under which I would be employed. 'You'll have holidays, time off, and so on. We will fix your retainer to cover all your living expenses – rent, that sort of thing. Then we will also pay any expenses that the work involves – train fares, petrol, meals on the way. You'll have to keep good records!'

There were quite a few details to be sorted out, the kind that have to be dealt with when you start any new job. But it wasn't all paperwork and business. There was a wonderful sense of embarking on a new venture, a new stage of God's work.

'We believe that God has raised you up for a purpose,' said Sylvia Mary gently. 'We are very sure of God's leading in this.'

It was a sobering and joyous thought. But it wasn't earthshaking or mind-blowing. God has a plan for all of us. He hears us when we ask him for guidance. He answers prayer. So why should we be surprised, when he makes his plans known? My chief feeling at that time was gratitude to him for making it so clear to me, so soon. I know that sometimes he chooses to wait before answering prayer. He waited two years before he opened the gates of Lard Yao in answer to my prayers and those of thousands who were praying for me – and I can see many reasons why I can thank him for waiting. But when I prayed about joining the staff of the Fellowship, he gave me my answer very quickly, so that I never had any doubts at all.

'What do we do now?' I asked them. 'What's the next step?'

'Well,' said Mary, 'firstly we need to know what you need to live on.'

The retainer which was finally settled on was rather more than the £17 I had been receiving from the State Supplementary Benefit scheme. Many Christian organisations are unable to pay salaries equivalent to those paid in secular firms for similar work, and those who choose to work for them do so knowing that they will never become rich! But I was not poor working for Prison Christian Fellowship, and never have been.

That settled, the next question was: what exactly should I be doing in my day-to-day work for the Fellowship? That too we decided to allow to shape itself as we asked the Lord for his help in planning this new development.

To begin with I travelled round some of the local regions of Prison Christian Fellowship with Ross. We went to Durham, Bedford and Liverpool, and Ross explained that this would help me to get to know how the Fellowship operated nationally and also would give opportunities for me to speak to local groups.

'But what do you want me to *do*?' I asked Ross.

'Just share with people. Share your testimony, tell people what God has done in your life. Tell them about what it's like in prison, and the needs there are there.'

By now I knew quite a lot about Prison Christian Fellowship. I was fired with enthusiasm by the fact that in America it wasn't an enormous operation run from an impressive headquarters. I'd caught the vision of a movement that was made up of individuals in local groups, ordinary Christians involved in local prisons by praying and visiting. This was what the Fellowship in England was engaged in building up, and this was what I was to be involved in.

In those early days the pattern of meetings was quickly established. Ross would begin by explaining how Prison Christian Fellowship began in Britain, and about the American organisation and Chuck Colson's original vision. Then I would share my own experiences, which illustrated the prisoner's point of view. I talked about what it was like, as a prisoner, to be visited by Christians – about Lucille's faithful visits, about Margaret and Martha Livesey. The thing about Lucille, I pointed out, was that she wasn't an expert, she'd had no training in prison visiting. She was a very ordinary person without special qualifications. And yet you don't need qualifications. You need love. God put it into Lucille's heart to minister to me in a special way, and though she had to put up with antagonism and bitterness for a long time, eventually God honoured her commitment and I became a Christian.

I shared these and similar experiences with the groups that I visited with Ross. I wanted to encourage Christians, especially those who already had a longing for an opportunity to share the gospel with prisoners.

For some time I went to one meeting a week, or sometimes two in the same area on consecutive days. At the same time I remained a member of the Preston prayer group, and each month I shared with them what I'd been doing and the people I'd met. They prayed for me regularly and I was very grateful, because I knew that it made such a difference, just as the prayers of the congregation at St. Andrews made a difference.

Though at first I only had a couple of engagements a week, it meant that I had to be away from home more and more. A local Methodist minister, Albert Greasley, helped me with the correspondence and the invitations which were beginning to come in as word spread that I was now on the staff. Groups who had prayed for me, or who had read my story in the newspapers since my release, wrote to ask if I could go and speak to them, and because mine was still a comparatively recent front-page story, it meant that people who weren't Christians or who weren't previously involved in the group would be willing to come along. So it wasn't long before I had a programme of my own to follow instead of accompanying Ross on his rounds.

John Harris organised the London office. At first I found myself telephoning him frequently. 'John, please – tell me what I'm supposed to be doing!'

I never had a formally-stated job specification; few people in Prison Christian Fellowship did. It took me some time to get used to the fact that I wasn't full-time with the Fellowship in the same way that one might be a full-time school teacher or shop assistant. I was a representative, retained to help Prison Christian Fellowship by speaking to groups and individuals, presenting the Fellowship's work to local churches, and being available in whatever capacities might be helpful in the work. I reported regularly on what I had been doing, to Ross and to John, but nobody kept an hour-by-hour check on my activities.

Many of the speaking invitations I received when I first started work were sent to me personally, because people knew who I was from the newspapers and the various broadcasts, but not many knew that I was with the Fellowship. We resolved this by deciding that the gifts of money which were often given to me after I had spoken at a meeting would be passed direct to the London office and used for the Fellowship's work, and from the London office I would receive my monthly retainer and my travelling expenses. It was a good arrangement which worked well.

Ross Simpson became a trusted friend and advisor, and I benefited from his experience as a speaker and as a representative of Prison Christian Fellowship.

I had never worked with anybody like him before. He was an open, warm-hearted man who tended to include the Lord in conversations with other people. 'Thank you, Lord!' he would say, or 'Praise the Lord!', when something worked out well. He never said it in a particularly 'holy' way; it was as if he was addressing somebody as much in the same room as I was but who happened to be invisible. Working with Ross I learned an enormous amount about talking to groups, dealing with questions, and ministering to people's needs. I also found my faith reinforced as Ross constantly praised and thanked the Lord.

In January I heard that Chris, the cheerful Dutch blonde with whom I'd been friends in Lard Yao, had been released. In her letter to me she gave me her telephone number in Holland, and I telephoned her as soon as she got back. We

146

had a crazy conversation, just like the ones I'd had with people just after I'd got back to England, and we promised each other we'd meet up as soon as we could.

For the present I had enough to come to grips with in England. Apart from anything else I was beginning to feel a little bit guilty about June. I wondered whether it might seem that I was going to get wrapped up in my new interests and leave her more and more on her own. June had her own life, of course, with an interesting job and lots of friends, but we'd become very close since Mum died, and I didn't want her to feel that I'd only been passing the time until something exciting came along. But I need not have worried, because June was marvellous. She didn't resent my frequent absences and increasingly unpredictable timetable; she was happy for me that I had found something I really wanted to do, because we'd discussed the future together and my need for a job.

Though my week now revolved around my speaking engagements, I didn't spend all my time working. I went out with June quite often, and had friends in church and outside. There wasn't time to have a hectic social life, but neither did I have my nose to the grindstone all the time.

One evening late in January I went with June to the twenty-first birthday party of one of her friends from work. I was tired and a bit depressed; one of the reasons I'd gone out that evening was to cheer myself up.

We arrived early and were sitting waiting for the others to arrive when a male voice behind me said, 'Hello, Rita!' It was the kind of enthusiastic greeting that you would normally expect from a long-lost relative.

I looked round. The speaker was a good-looking man about my own age. I didn't recognise him. 'Hello,' I said reluctantly.

'Don't you remember me? I went to school with you. You remember me.'

I looked at him sceptically. 'Come off it,' I said severely.

'You don't know me from school. You know me from the newspaper.' I was still sensitive about the fact that people started at me when I went out of the house, and I had become expert at fending off men who thought that because I had worked in a Hong Kong night club I might be easier to charm than other girls.

He looked disconcerted. 'No, really, I went to school with you. We went to St. Wilfrid's together.' June watched in amusement.

'Oh yes?' I challenged, still unconvinced. 'Well then, what's your name?'

'Trevor Carroll,' he replied.

I gulped. 'You were in the football team.'

He sat down. 'Of course I was.'

We began chatting. After a while other people arrived and the party got under way. Trevor said, 'Would you like an evening out some time?'

'I'd love it,' I replied. I'd enjoyed being with him.

'I work nights so I'm not always free in the evening, but what about Saturday?'

My face fell. I was away that weekend on a visit for the Fellowship. 'I can't make it.'

'How about Friday?'

'Oh – I'm afraid I'm due in Liverpool on Friday . . .'

I think anyone else might have given up at that point, but Trevor persisted. 'The following Monday?'

'I'm free that night,' I grinned.

Trevor was fun, and I had a really enjoyable time with him that Monday. What I liked about him especially was that even on that first date he didn't try to press me for details of my Thailand experience. He just didn't mention it. I'd been asked out several times since I returned from Lard Yao, but the conversation had invariably turned to prison, and that had spoiled things. I wanted to feel that I was worth talking to on my own account, not just because I had been in the newspapers.

I began seeing him from time to time, though there wasn't much opportunity for regular meetings while I was working away from home increasingly and Trevor worked his night shifts. But we met when we could. I found myself liking him more and more, and began to wonder where it might lead. I started to pray about him, asking the Lord to guide me in that part of my life just as he had in all the others.

15: Into Prisons

We are pleased to inform you that Rita Nightingale has agreed to undertake ministry on behalf of PCF and is available for the following: 1. Public/Church meetings; 2. Prison visits; 3. Seminar work.

Prison Christian Fellowship, *Regional and Development News* (Spring 1981)

From my first days in Prison Christian Fellowship, I prayed before every meeting I attended and every talk I gave. As my workload grew I found that I had to pray about which invitations I was going to accept and which decline. It was becoming physically impossible to accept them all, for reasons of time if for no other. As each invitation was forwarded to me by Albert Greasley it had to be talked over with Ross. What group was it? What part of the country was it in – did it fit in with my movements at that time? What were the needs of the group in question? Then we would pray about it together and make a decision on whether I should accept or decline.

My 1981 diary shows an increasing number of speaking engagements in all parts of the country. In addition, my personal mail was increasing. In January, for example, I received a letter from an American prisoner who had been on Death Row for three years. He had seen my photograph and an accompanying article in the Prison Fellowship Newsletter. I received many letters from America, from prisoners who had read my story or had heard tapes.

The meetings I attended in those early months were of several different kinds. One of the most important tasks I had was helping to encourage the growth of the small Prison Christian Fellowship 'core groups' which Sylvia Mary described in the Spring 1981 newsletter:

> Most exciting to me has been the gathering together in 13 different areas, covering 29 prisons, of the body of Christ to pray for prison and prisoners in those areas and to help prisoners in practical ways. These areas have been set up by Ross Simpson, our Regional Director, and John Harris, our Administrator, initially . . . The first principle is that a small core group, brothers and sisters in Christ, meet to pray together and to take on the responsibility for collecting together the Christians in that area.

After my American visit, and particularly after the week I spent with the girls on the discipleship course, I came back inspired with the vision of how it might be in England. The small regional groups were considered very important by us all. We knew the power of prayer, we'd proved it in our own lives. We knew that if the Lord so chose he could take the groups and build a mighty network of praying Christians, and use them to reach into prisons and transform the lives of prisoners.

Prisoners, of course, were the focus of the Fellowship's work, and almost as soon as I joined the staff I began to visit prisons with Ross. There was not now a problem of access, and I made my first prison visit – to a women's prison in the North of England – in January.

I'm not sure what I was expecting, though I was aware that the frequent cosy television and film portrayal of prison as a jolly rogue's club was a glamourisation. Beyond that I had nothing to prepare me in advance.

We went in through a heavily-secured gate, and were taken into a dreary stone corridor with iron walkways which clanged when people walked along them. Every hundred yards or so there was a rusty stain down the wall where the iron pipes that ran the length of the walls had leaked. There was a feeling of dampness in the air, and though there were radiators, I shivered.

I was shocked by what I saw. After Lard Yao I'd had high hopes of British prisons – for a while it had seemed I might be transferred to one – but I'd reckoned without the overcrowding. The best and most enlightened governors often struggle unsuccessfully with the problem. It is a matter of simple mathematics; a prison can hold only a certain number of inmates comfortably. Buildings that are used by a lot of people suffer, and so do the people. In many chamber-pots are still used because of the queues for bathroom facilities in the morning. Though I usually visit the prisons later in the day and there's no noticeable trace left by then, I have been told that there's a characteristic and unpleasant smell that hangs around the corridors of such prisons first thing in the morning.

A prison officer took charge of us. 'Follow me,' she said politely, and led us to the room where the meeting was to be held. Her face was virtually expressionless; most of the staff in that prison were severe and unbending, and their aloofness contributed substantially to the frigid atmosphere. The room she took us to was in the basement. It was a stone-walled, fairly large interview room. Guards with immobile faces stood at the door and watched us incuriously.

The scenes inside the prison did not arouse in me any vivid memories of Lard Yao. One reason, I suppose, is that prisons in the West are very different. When I go into an English prison there's very little that I see there to physically remind me of Lard Yao. But a stronger reason is that whenever I am in a prison talking to the prisoners, when I get into conversation with individuals and small groups, I don't think about whether it's a good one or a bad one. Of course I'm aware that I'm in a cell or a prison meeting room, but I know from my own experience that when you're a prisoner who's become a Christian, what hurts is not the environment but the sight of your visitors leaving. It's the lack of freedom, not the colour of paintwork that hurts.

If you are a believer serving a prison sentence, you feel wonderful when Christian visitors come in from outside. You have a great time sharing with them and praying with them. You are on a spiritual 'high'. Then your visitors leave, and you go back to your cell and they go to wherever they choose, and you slump.

That's why I always try to encourage people who are in prison. I know how they are going to feel after I've gone. 'Yes, I really know how you're rejoicing now, it's great, the Lord is blessing us as we meet here together; but after we've gone and you're on your own, *hold on* to this. Because this is reality, not the other. God is giving us the joy of his presence now, but he won't take that from you when we go.'

I made many prison visits and got to know prisoners in different parts of the country. Sometimes we spoke to large groups, sometimes to three or four. As a result my mail continued to increase. Prisoners wrote regularly.

In work with prisoners, keeping up with one's correspondence is a major task. For most people serving sentences, visiting time is all too short and letters are a very real window onto the outside world. Some prisoners have broken marriages or have been disowned by their families, and when a sympathetic visitor writes to them, the reply fills page after page of prison notepaper.

153

The sight of the ruled sheets, with the sender's name and institution written at the top among the censor's stamps and the official reference numbers, moved me profoundly. There are not many more obvious symbols of the loss of freedom that prison entails. In their letters as in daily life, the inmates are regimented and organised. 'Prisoners should only write below this line' is printed firmly across the top of the sheet. Below, the handwriting often sprawls and slants as if struggling to escape the cramped ruled lines on which regulations insist the letter be written.

All the letters had to be read and prayed over. Answers could never be superficial. Clearly some of the prisoners were writing merely to pass away a half hour, raising clever theological points and challenging me to provide an answer. But the apparently sarcastic jibe about evolution or the authority of the Bible might conceal a real hunger to know. Somebody was waiting anxiously to receive your response to the fear expressed or the spiritual problem raised. It might well be of crucial importance to the prisoner who had written.

Some of the letters were heartbreakingly sad.

> I sit and wonder sometimes [wrote one prisoner] what life is really like without prison and how good it would be to live a good and holy life without ever doing wrong again . . .

I answered them all with much prayer.

As the year progressed I became increasingly involved in my new work. I continued to see Trevor, and we enjoyed each other's company more and more. Also I still wrote to Hannah and the girls in Lard Yao and to my friends in America, and I telephoned Chris in Holland quite often.

In March, June and I went to Holland to visit her. It was a madcap week. We enjoyed sightseeing in Amsterdam, but for most of the time Chris and I were reminiscing about prison, shrieking with laughter as we recalled some escapade or other, and talking endlessly about the people we'd known there and the things we'd done.

'You know,' June said to us in some amazement, 'anybody would think you'd been on holiday in Bangkok all that time, the way you go on about it.'

Chris looked at me, and we burst out laughing. It was true; we'd laughed and giggled about most of our reminiscences, and if one shouted a Thai word to the other it was a cue for instant merriment. June must have thought we'd had an incredible time together.

We hadn't, of course. It's just that you remember the good times. There were lots of bright moments in Lard Yao, and funny things did happen. But that wasn't what prison was about. If I were able to remember the bad times with such clarity, I doubt if I would sleep at nights.

After five days we said goodbye with regret, and June and I returned home.

A month later, I got down from the coach at Victoria coach station in London and looked around the crowds. I had arranged to meet somebody there. We were going to discuss writing a book together.

Although I had resolutely refused to sell my story to the newspapers, a book seemed a very different matter. When people heard me speaking about what had happened to me in prison, they often asked me whether I had written a book. I could see that having control of how the story was written would be a different matter from allowing the possibility of newspaper distortion and sensationalism. I had read Chuck Colson's two books *Born Again* and *Life Sentence*, and I knew the power of such books. Thousands who had never heard Chuck speak had had their lives changed by his writings. If God wanted me to write a book, I knew that God would use it.

Meetings with publishers had been part of my itinerary when I was in America.

'I don't know whether I *could* write a book,' I had admitted to Chuck Colson. 'I've never done anything like that at all.'

He explained to me that many successful books had been produced by somebody with a story to tell working with somebody who had the ability to write – it was called 'ghost writing'. A number of the most widely-read Christian books of recent years had in fact been written by one husband-and-wife team of ghost writers, John and Elizabeth Sherrill.

I remembered seeing their names on the title pages of books I'd read since I became a Christian. They'd collaborated with Corrie ten Boom on *The Hiding Place*, with Brother Andrew on *God's Smuggler*, and with several more authors I'd read. They'd also given Chuck Colson a tremendous amount of help with *Born Again*, and as publishers had been closely involved with *Life Sentence*. 'Find somebody you can work with, and you'll find you will be able to produce a book,' advised Chuck.

He arranged meetings with several publishers. They were much more approachable than I had expected, and I enjoyed the discussions. It was agreed that a ghost writer would be a good idea, and several names were suggested.

In the end, however, I came to the decision that I wanted to work with an English writer. 'It's not that I think the American writers couldn't do it, it's not that at all,' I explained. 'But I'm English, you know? That's where my roots are. I'd really like to find somebody in England, if I could.'

Chuck, who had put in a good deal of work on my behalf setting up the meetings, was understanding. 'Well,' he said, 'make sure you get good advice when you get home.' He reached for an address book. 'Contact Edward England. He's a literary agent. I've known him for years. He'll look after you.'

Back in Blackburn, I received a letter from Edward

England. Chuck had telephoned him and told him he had discussed a possible book with me. Edward arranged for me to meet David Porter, a Christian freelance writer who had written several books, and in April I arrived at Victoria coach station to meet him.

We liked each other immediately, and decided very quickly that we would be able to work with each other. Edward arranged for us to meet a publisher and the formalities were rapidly dealt with. Over the next few months we met several times, either in Blackburn or at David's cottage in Hampshire, and armed with a tape recorder and notebook David set about the task of setting down my story.

It was a strange experience. I was having to think about things that I hadn't thought about for a long time. There were tearful times and hilarious times, as I relived the sad moments and the good ones. Slowly we put together a first draft, often working late into the night to make the most of a few days snatched from crowded schedules. As the story took shape, I, David and his wife Tricia became good friends.

The work of Prison Christian Fellowship during my first year expanded in a number of directions. The Trustees launched a number of new activities. Courses for voluntary helpers were started, designed to give a basic grounding in work with prisoners and an orientation for those who, all over the country, were contemplating offering themselves as volunteers in various ways. 'Breakthrough '81' was a project that linked many of the prisons and borstals in the South of England, and, like all the Fellowship's activities, relied heavily on committed prayer support. 'Springboard' was the title given to a study series intended to give discipleship training to prisoners, and was a first step in planning seminars out of prison, such as I had attended in Washington, and which the Fellowship was praying might happen in England before long.

When I look through my 1981 diary I find that I was involved with many of these and other exciting projects. It was a time of growth for the Fellowship and for me as well. The Lord looked after me throughout, providing me with the fellowship and support of my church, plentiful help and counsel from my colleagues, Trevor's friendship, a great deal of spiritual satisfaction from what I was doing and a fortnight's summer holiday in Spain with June, when I lazed on the beach, contemplated the cloudless sky, and forgot all about work and travelling around the country.

16: Shepherds

*'New lives for old' has been our theme, and
it is being proved true day by day here as
men find for themselves the power of the
Risen Lord.*

Strangeways Prison prayer letter, May
1984

In the pub a man was gazing at me, his mouth open. His
head was framed in the hatch that separated the two bars.
We'd come in for a meal. All round, people were chatting,
coming and going, ordering food and drinks. In the hubbub
the man continued to stare at me, oblivious to what was
going on.

I nudged Trevor. 'It's because I'm so gorgeous,' I
laughed. We both turned deliberately to face the man and
stared back. I waited for him to blush and turn away. He
continued his openmouthed, unvarying gaze.

Trevor crossed the room and confronted him. 'What are
you looking at? What's so interesting?'

The man transferred his gaze to Trevor for a moment and
then looked back at me. He didn't say a word.

We moved out of his line of sight. I sighed.'It still
happens a lot, Trevor. Even now. People remember I was
the one in the papers. Sorry.'

I did enjoy being with Trevor, with or without publicity. He was a quiet person, unruffled by the fact that I was liable to disappear at a moment's notice and ring up from Dartmoor or Glasgow to tell him I'd just spent the evening in the local prison. He wasn't part of Prison Christian Fellowship, and he didn't go to St. Andrew's. He was somebody outside the new and exciting life I was leading, and because of that I could relax when I was with him in a way that was otherwise very difficult.

As I began to realise that he was becoming fond of me, and I was growing closer to him, I prayed about our relationship. Trevor wasn't the sort of person to talk much about religion. He had his own beliefs and he thought deeply, but he disliked over-enthusiasm in any shape or form. We talked about Christianity a great deal, even in the process of me telling him what I'd been doing between our dates. Trevor believed very strongly in a personal God, and he had a churchgoing background. The fact that he didn't shout about his beliefs didn't mean that he had none.

I knew all the arguments about having non-Christian boyfriends, and I could see their validity; but to me Trevor wasn't a non-Christian. He gave me a lot of strength, and some of that strength was spiritual strength. We prayed together and shared my vision for prisoners, and all that was an important part of our relationship. On the other hand, I had real doubts. I wasn't sure whether it would be right to move forward in the relationship. Trevor was unique, he wasn't like any Christian I knew. I wanted to be sure, and I wanted us both to be sure. So I continued to pray.

I was really beginning to enjoy the variety in the work I was doing. One day I might be speaking to a tiny group, a few interested people who'd come together to discuss the starting of a Prison Christian Fellowship prayer group in a remote part of the country; a few days later, I might be speaking to a crowd of several hundred. I was speaking to audiences of all ages, from children's groups to old age pensioners. I spoke at organisations like the Christian Police Association and groups of Christian lawyers.

Sometimes I caught myself thinking, *What am I doing here?* I had very little in common with the members of many of the groups I spoke to, though they were usually very kind to me. Apart from Christ, I had absolutely nothing in common with some of them. Yet God had put me in those situations to share something of what he had done in my life.

The size of a group has never bothered me. In a prison situation I would rather talk to a small group than a large one. I thank God for every opportunity I get to be with prisoners, but there is a difference between talking *at* a group, say in a ten-minute spot in a Sunday morning chapel service, and talking *with* a group. In a chaplain's hour or a discussion group the conversation is two-way. The people in the group haven't come to prison because they wanted to, but they've come to the group because they're Christians, and that gives you a tremendous basis for sharing. You can ask them questions, you can be interrupted, you can change the direction of what you're saying as you begin to get to know the needs of the different members of the group. You can't do that in a formal service, where you just have to pray that the Lord will prepare you with something that will be helpful to the listeners.

Something that I learned very rapidly from working with Ross and John was the fact that the prison chaplain is a key factor in the work of the Fellowship. Today links have been established with many of them. His is a very exposed role. He is in the prison to help people to find Christ.

I've been saddened in my travels when I have asked church groups, 'How many of you ever pray for your local prison chaplain?' Even in churches which have prisons in their locality, it's rare to find believers taking on the burden of supporting the chaplains in prayer. If you have no time or opportunity to help prisoners in any other way – pray for the chaplains! God has put them in the prisons to reveal him to those who are locked inside.

The chaplain is invariably overworked. He has administrative duties which would take up a large part of anybody's working week, and then he has a pastoral duty to the prisoners to whom he ministers. As well as being available for spiritual counselling, in many prisons he has the task of interviewing every prisoner on arrival and discovering any domestic problems that need to be taken care of over a period of time.

It's the kind of job that you never get on top of, because the scope is limitless. The Sunday service, which is the aspect of prison religious life of which the public is usually most aware (through television and film portrayals of prison life), is only a small part of his responsibilities, and an effective prison chaplain will find he has to earmark precious time even to prepare for that.

The policy of Prison Christian Fellowship has always been to work through the chaplains, who are approached for permission to enter the prison. In my own case, for example, I was from the start invited into prisons either because the chaplain himself had heard of me and invited me himself, or because Prison Christian Fellowship had written to say that I would be in the region at a certain time and would be able to visit the prison if required.

In some prisons, I discovered, the chaplain organises several activities each week. There are Bible studies, chaplain's hour, discussion groups, and other opportunities for prisoners who want to find out about Christianity. Some inmates are Christians already, having got into trouble since their conversion or having become Christians in prison. In either case, the ministry within prisons is vitally important.

And in prisons all over the country (and all over the world) Prison Christian Fellowship is seeing that ministry growing and expanding as the Lord brings men into the prison service who long to bring prisoners to him, and as he brings to maturity the patient work of chaplains who have struggled for years and, until recently, seen little fruit of their labours.

The Holy Spirit is on the move in the prisons!

Strangeways Prison is a good example. It was one of the first prisons that I visited. I had heard a lot about it because it had some television attention. Like many British prisons, it has a severe overcrowding problem. That means that the chaplain's workload is much heavier, because more people need individual attention.

Yet God is doing wonderful things in that prison. Noel Proctor, a chaplain there, has seen miraculous things happen. Lives have been changed, apparently insuperable problems have been swept away, hardened criminals have become radiant, caring Christians. There are no riots at Strangeways. So many people are becoming Christians that the chapel is filled three times over on Sundays.

Noel is adamant that the credit does not belong to him. He points to his team of colleagues in the prison, and to the great numbers of people outside who pray regularly and specifically for the needs of Strangeways. The local branch of Prison Christian Fellowship prays, and also circulates a prayerletter to 2,000 praying Christians. The Holy Spirit has honoured these prayers and has used the labours of the Christian team in the prison. The results have been astonishing.

That's a good illustration of the vision for Prison Christian Fellowship. Local Christians, praying for their local prison situation; and beyond that, becoming a fellowship such that when prisoners are released they can be told. 'Look, here is a group of Christians who are from all sorts of backgrounds and who know where you've been. You can link up with them and continue to grow in your Christian faith, while you decide what to do next.'

So I continued in the work of helping local groups and visiting in prisons. Ross and John were always available for help and a shoulder to cry on. There were times when I felt bitterly discouraged, and sometimes people were insensitive and even unkind. At those times I knew I could count on the wisdom and support of Ross, John, Herrick Daniels, Tom Marriot (another Prison Christian Fellowship worker with whom I had made good friends), Tony Ralls in Devon, Trevor, and a number of others.

I was finding it difficult to adjust to becoming a full-time speaker. I was now speaking much more than the one or two meetings a week that I had been allocated when I began. I'd never envisaged that happening, and it gave me some problems.

There were aspects of speaking in public that thrilled me. For example, I never tired of telling my own story, because it was always new to the people I was sharing it with, and it was a way of telling people who God could do for them. Essentially, what happened to me in Thailand happens to everyone who becomes a Christian. We're all the same inside. We are all conscious of an emptiness within ourselves, we try to fill the gap. The void in my own life had nothing to do with prison. It was there before I was arrested. When I had fine clothes, an exotic job, a handsome boyfriend who lavished gifts and money on me – I used to cry myself to sleep at night. Prison wasn't the problem. Prison was where I found out how the problem had been solved for me, two thousand years ago.

I was sometimes in situations, like in America, where I would be speaking at two or three meetings in a single day, and each time giving basically the same message. I had to remind myself: *Don't let it become automatic*. But it didn't, because I prayed that the Holy Spirit would reveal to me what each audience needed, and I would adjust my talk to be relevant. Usually I spoke for about half my time about Lard Yao and the rest about Prison Fellowship, but I varied it each time. If I thought that a number of the audiences were not Christians I'd emphasise Lard Yao and give a gospel address, and so on.

Problems arose in certain situations, like the occasion where I spoke to a very large audience, and it was like talking to a mattress. Nothing came back, no warmth, no response, nothing.

As I spoke I began to resent these people. Speaking is something that is very emotional for me. I'm talking about crises in my life, giving a large part of myself to the audience; and it hurts to sense no answering sympathy.

I finished my talk and afterwards stood at the door, and people shook hands as they went out. Most of them made some sort of polite comment. When a large lady approached and extended her hand I expected her to do the same. By that time I was feeling very depressed and just wanted to leave.

'Oh, Rita!' she said enthusiastically, grasping my hand and squeezing it. 'That was such a *lovely* story!'

I was so upset that I almost smacked her hand away. 'It *isn't* a story,' I retorted, and then retrieved my polite smile and shook hands properly. Inwardly I was fuming. *What's the point of talking to these people? You can lay it on the line what Christian commitment is, and it rolls right over their heads.*

When I got home I complained to God. *Lord, I'm not doing any more of this stuff. You saw what happened tonight. I'm sticking with the prisoners, who need to hear about you.*

Almost there and then, I felt an overpowering conviction that I had been totally in the wrong. *Who are you, to decide what has gone in and what hasn't? This is what I want you to do, and I want you to do it whether you get any encouragement or not.*

I went to Ross and told him about it, and he was very

supportive, but I had learned an important lesson from the experience. If you do a lot of speaking in public you quite often find an audience that seems to be taking in nothing of what you're saying. But I have discovered that it's often in just such meetings that God is really dealing with somebody, or that the meeting marked a breakthrough in the life of some present.

17: Discouragements and Encouragements

I feel deeply that I must change my life for
the better . . . please can you send me some
Scripture leaflets.

Letter from a prisoner.

By Spring 1982, Albert Greasley, who had taken on the work of keeping my diary even though he had other commitments, was no longer able to devote the necessary time to the task because of other pressures. I was very grateful to him for what he had done, and it didn't mean that I was left without help because a few months later Christine Austin joined the London office staff of Prison Christian Fellowship.

Christine and her husband Brian had been involved with work among young people for several years, and were already supporters of Prison Christian Fellowship. Among other responsibilities, she took over the organisation of my appointments, and I was able to channel invitations through her.

I continued to work in the two main areas of speaking to Fellowship groups and other Christian gatherings, and of going into prisons to share with the prisoners. It was very humbling to see the hand of God working in all sorts of situations.

My correspondence files contain many evidences of God at work in the prisons. 'I have a very nice church visitor,' wrote one man, ' – now a personal friend, who comes in to see me every fortnight, and we do discuss a lot about belief and faith . . .' Another writes, 'I try my best, though sometimes I fail. What saves me is the fact that occasionally I get brief "flashes of light" (metaphorically speaking) in which I feel the Lord's hands upon me and on those occasions my faith is like the hardest granite.'

Many of the Christian men and women have been coming to Bible studies and sharing groups for as long as I have been working in prisons. We've seen wonderful instances of people growing incredibly strong in the Lord, and developing real gifts of leadership and understanding. We've seen prisoners converted by the testimony of other prisoners. We've had amazing encouragements.

But there are disappointments as well. I think, for example, of a man who used to come to a group in a prison which I visited regularly. Over a number of meetings I and other members of Prison Christian Fellowship came to know him well. He was just coming to the end of a major sentence when I first met him, and I was sure his commitment to Christ was genuine.

Eighteen months after he left prison he had found a home with a Christian family, he had a job, and he sometimes gave his testimony in public and spoke of how the Lord had changed his life. Then he suddenly disappeared. He left the house in which he lived, and gave no indication of where he was going. We lost touch with him completely, and the follow up group that was involved with him could do nothing but pray.

Much later, we heard of him again. He was back in prison in the South of England.

How do you cope with a disappointment like that? You can write the man off, say that his conversion was a sham; and there's no doubt that some Christians who observed the whole sequence of events have assumed that this was so. Or you can simply accept that discouragement is part of the Christian life, that often things do not turn out as we would have expected. And you start back at the beginning, going to him where he is and seeking to share the love of Christ with him all over again.

Many times, in such situations, I remembered my Mum. How many questions I asked when she became ill, and how many of them remained unanswered! Yet I knew the Lord was in control. And in the same way I was able to pray for that man. I may never know the end of the story. But God does.

Yet nothing can destroy what God is building in the prisons, and so many times, we are privileged to see God revealing part of what he is doing. There are tremendous encouragements as well as disappointments. One of the most wonderful visits I have made with Prison Fellowship was to Northern Ireland.

When I arrived in Ulster with Ross Simpson in October 1982 it was the first time I had ever visited the province. We flew across one damp and misty day, and we were due to go to the notorious H-Blocks to meet with a small group of Christian prisoners. Soon several of us were packed into a small van driving down a tarmac road towards the main prison block, through drizzling rain and a succession of checkpoints.

The sight of armed men, uniforms, and the grey prison blocks rearing dismally ahead filled me with a dread that verged on panic. It was like a black-and-white film of the Second World War, with that same colourless hopelessness that ruled out the possibility that any normal life existed outside. It would not have surprised me to have seen such a a place in the Soviet Union, but it was a shock to see it in Britain. *What am I going to say to these men?*, I thought. *What have I got to offer them?*

In a way that's a good reaction. I experience it almost every time I speak in public, and it's helpful to me, because it reminds me that what is important isn't so much what I have to say but what the Lord is going to say through me. But that day it was an almost totally depressing feeling, as if a dull black cloud was hovering over my head as I went into the building.

We went down long bare corridors with cells leading off them, and all around us we could hear shouted conversation and the other sounds of prison life. We were shown into a tiny room, and Ross and I sat and waited with a couple of people from Prison Fellowship Northern Ireland (which is a separately chartered group – with which the London-based organisation works very closely – within Prison Fellowship International).

One by one the men filed in. They sat down quietly in a circle. There were about ten of them. Somebody sitting near me coughed and said quietly, 'Well; let's begin with prayer.'

He led us in a simple prayer. He prayed for other prisoners and for prison officers by name. He prayed that God's power would be present in that prison and touch the lives of all inside. As he prayed I wept. It wasn't so much what he said, it was the overwhelming sense of the presence of God in that small room. We were surrounded by the din of prison, but in that circle there was a peace and quietness which you could almost touch.

We were able to spend an hour with the group. I spoke for a short time, and so did Ross, and the men shared with us, talking about what the Lord had done for them in prison. Afterwards I was told something of the man who had prayed. He was inside for the most appalling crimes. The things he'd done terrified me. But he had become a Christian in prison.

I got into conversation with him, and I asked him a question I don't very often ask. 'How did you become a Christian?'

He told me the story of his conversion. He'd gone to a Prison Fellowship open meeting in the prison. It had sounded good for a laugh and he was bored.

'So I sat at the back. Then I saw a woman sitting at the front and I recognised her. I was a member of the IRA, and we'd shot her husband. She was a police widow, only twenty-eight, with two or three young kids.'

He swallowed, and went on, 'We were a mixed lot in that audience, a lot of us were in the IRA. And this woman – I couldn't believe it! She knew who we were, oh, she knew, and she stood up in front of us and she said, "I just want to say that if any of you have any relatives or friends who'd like to come out to visit you here, let me know and I'll be only too glad to arrange it."'

He looked at me squarely. 'It hit me hard, right deep inside me. How could she say that? Members of my organisation shot her husband dead, left her on her own with kids. And she could stand up and say something like that . . . '

He'd gone up to her at the end of the meeting and challenged her to explain why she had said what she'd said. So she shared the love of Jesus with him. She told him what he'd done in her life, how she had found the strength to forgive.

'That was how I became a Christian,' he told me quietly.

Back in England I told Trevor what had happened. 'I'm never going to make judgements again,' I said. And I really have tried not to. It's too easy to categorise, to assign blame according to easy formulae. God isn't like that. One of the most amazing prayer meetings I have been to in Northern Ireland was in a Catholic stronghold, and it consisted entirely of Catholic women. Before I went to Northern Ireland I'd assumed I would tend to sympathise with the

Protestant political position, but over there, I've shared platforms with Christians from both sides.

I spoke at several meetings with Liam McCloskey, who was one of the IRA hunger strikers. He was convicted of terrorist crimes, and he went on hunger strike as part of the IRA campaign for their prisoners to be given 'political prisoner' status. He almost died, he was blind from starvation, and it was only because he was under age that his mother was able to persuade the authorities to force-feed him. Liam became a Christian, and when he was on parole we both gave our testimonies at a number of churches.

It's a continuing sadness to me to see that bigotry and intolerance not only appear on both sides of the Northern Ireland divide, but also infect individual Christians. I will never forget one meeting during that visit, at which Liam and I had been giving our testimonies. It was a Protestant church, and afterwards I went downstairs to a room where tea was being served.

A small group had surrounded Liam and were arguing with him. I wandered across to eavesdrop. I could hardly believe what they were saying to him.

'How can you possibly call yourself a Christian,' one was saying forcefully, 'while you're still going to the Catholic Church?'

The shock was almost physical. I felt I'd been punched in the midriff. I'd had my eyes opened to the fact that to such people, Christianity and Catholicism are mutually incompatible. Of course there is intolerance on both sides, and I've met Catholic Christians who feel similarly about Protestants.

I don't believe that the differences between Protestants and Roman Catholics are trivial, nor that they are not evidence of different views of the Bible which must eventually be sorted out. Neither do I believe that the long history of troubles in the tragic communities of Northern

Ireland have no basis in fact or that there are not real problems to be dealt with if the province is to have political peace again. What I do believe is that the Holy Spirit is moving through Northern Ireland. He is transforming individual lives and whole communities. He is kindling love in peoples' hearts where once only hatred burned. In peoples' homes, in the streets, in the prison cells, the Spirit's work is bearing fruit. Men and women are becoming Christians. They don't sort out all their problems immediately. Sometimes God heals wounds and wrong attitudes over a period of time. But the change that takes place in the heart is immediate, and what these new, born-again brothers and sisters need is the love and the support of local Christians. That is what Prison Christian Fellowship, along with many other Christian groups in the province, seeks to offer. We have been so blessed in seeing what God has done.

The other major event of October was the publication of *Freed for Life*. Our months of snatched days working on the book had born fruit. The publishers, Marshalls, held a press launch in the Church of St. Bride's in Fleet Street. It was a lovely occasion, when Ross, John, Sylvia Mary and several of my colleagues from Prison Fellowship were present. David and Tricia came up from Hampshire and afterwards Marshalls took us for a celebratory dinner.

The press were very kind to the book in their reviews. Plans were well advanced for an American edition by Tyndale House Publishers, and in Britain it sold so well that it had entered the Christian best-seller lists by Christmas.

18. Blessings

*Your life has been adventurous, rewarding
and a blessing – what more could you ask?*

Letter from Margaret Cole, July 1983.

I realised that I was falling in love with Trevor. In so many
ways he supported me and fulfilled me. He was homely, but
not in a boring way. He was quite separate from the work I
was doing, and some people were concerned about that;
but for me he was ideal. He was interested in my work, and
he stimulated me to think about it in fresh ways, but while
other men I'd known would have been irritatingly in awe of
the fact that I worked with the wife of a Member of
Parliament and a member of Richard Nixon's presidential
team, Trevor tolerantly let me get on with it and didn't go
on and on about my colleagues.

I once persuaded him to accompany me to a radio station
where I was to give a broadcast talk. While I sat in the
studio in front of the microphone and talked, he watched
open-mouthed. Afterwards he shook his head incredu-
lously.

'You were amazing!' he said.

I smiled graciously. He grinned back. 'You just talked
and talked and talked – I've never seen you like that. You
were unstoppable. Just like Esther Rantzen . . .'

In so many ways he was right for me, and I believed I was right for him.

My workload increased dramatically after the publication of *Freed for Life*. Invitations to speak came flooding in. I discovered openings I had never heard of before — a Christian women's luncheon club, for example, which had local branches in towns all over the country. The book sold in large numbers in the prisons, and I often found that when I went to speak to a group for the first time, *Freed for Life* had gone before and paved the way.

In the London office, Christine's workload increased in step with mine, as she dealt with the mounting piles of invitations. We prayed very hard about which we should accept and which we would have to decline.

In May 1983 I went to America again, for a speaking tour to promote *Freed for Life* and to do deputation work for Prison Christian Fellowship, sharing with American audiences what God was doing in England. Before I left I prayed earnestly about my relationship with Trevor. I prayed, and others did too, that if it was right for us to become further involved, the Lord would make it very clear to me. I asked the Lord to reveal his will to us both while I was in America.

It was an exhilarating month, with many speaking engagements and the chance to renew old friendships and make new ones. Since my previous visit, the offices of Prison Christian Fellowship and Prison Fellowship International had separated for reasons of space. The International office was now in a house, occupying the downstairs rooms. The upper storey was used as a hospitality house for international visitors. Ferne Sanford was living there as a hostess, and she looked after me for the whole of my tour.

We took up our friendship where we'd left it since my last visit, and a couple of visits Ferne had made to England since then. We had a marvellous time. I don't have many close friends because of the life I've been leading; but Ferne is one of them, even though we don't see each other very often. She is a very special person in my life.

I missed Trevor dreadfully, and while I enjoyed the trip enormously (I visited Canada for two days at the very end and met Prison Fellowship groups there), I looked forward to getting back to England.

When I returned we set aside time to be together. We talked for hours. Trevor told me that while I had been away he had experienced a deepening of his faith. When he talked about it I realised that the Lord had given Trevor a very special time while I was away, and now had given me the sign I had asked for. From that time our relationship was different, deeper and more committed. Trevor suggested we go and look for an engagement ring. I said 'Yes!' immediately, and we set August 6, 1983 as the wedding date.

It was hard to get back into gear, after the American trip and our engagement. July, however, was a very special month. The first International Prison Fellowship conference took place in Belfast, Northern Ireland. Fifteen chartered countries were represented, and it was thrilling to hear the delegates speak about the situation in their national prisons. Many were similar to Lard Yao or worse.

So it came to our wedding day, when I walked up the aisle on my Uncle George's arm. Trevor's grandfather had died suddenly, and we decided not to have a honeymoon, but we had a perfect day and a lovely time in our new home. We had a small wedding, but were delighted that Ross and Sylvia Mary were able to come up and represent Prison Christian Fellowship. It was the first time that Ross had met my aunts, and he really enjoyed talking with them. Ferne Sandford was there. She had attended the Belfast conference and was able to stay on for the wedding. Many letters from friends all over the world arrived, with lovely messages. We were blissfully happy, and I had a long break of several weeks, so we were able to spend lots of time with each other.

When I returned to work, I was hectically busy. I entered upon a crowded timetable that often meant that I saw Trevor only briefly at weekends. In many ways it was a strain for both of us, but he was understanding and supportive. We went to church together when we could, and when we were alone the time I had with Trevor was all the more precious.

It could not go on in that way, of course. Part of it was due to the holiday backlog, but part was due to the success of the book. People said to me, 'Isn't it a problem that you're so well known and Trevor isn't?'

My reply was always the same. 'Of course not, because when we're together, I'm not well-known!'

After some months, we were delighted to discover that I was expecting a baby, and this hastened the plans of Prison Christian Fellowship to control my timetable and decline more invitations. Now that I had a date on which I was to go on maternity leave, we planned my timetable like a military operation. Invitations that allowed a logical trip without detours or horrendous connections were accepted; many more we regretfully had to decline, because the travelling involved wouldn't have been fair to the baby or its mother! Christine shielded me from as many distractions as possible, and arranged my bookings so that I had as much time as possible with Trevor. I really appreciated very much the concern that the Fellowship showed me at that time, and the efforts that were undertaken to ensure my wellbeing and that of our baby.

Ben was born in summer 1984. He is beautiful. Among the letters of congratulation we have received have been hundreds from prisoners.

Earlier in the year Edward England, David and I had been discussing the possibility of a sequel to *Freed for Life*. We'd been working on it as and when time permitted. When David rang to congratulate us on Ben's birth, he added a final comment.

'I've got a title for the sequel, by the way. How about *Freed for Ever*?'

19: Full Circle

Ain't it funny how you get to be
The last thing you ever dreamed you'd be . . .

'The preacher's song', by David Rees.[1]

Sometimes people ask me in what ways I think I have grown as a Christian since I was released from prison.

One very important realisation has been that Christianity isn't a rigid mould into which people fit. You don't have to do a particular job or be a particular person before God will accept you. He accepts us because of what Jesus has done, not because of what we have done. As I have come to realise that, it has helped me to relate to prisoners more on the basis of the unity that Christians have with each other in Christ, than on whether they say the 'right' things or have a view of God identical to mine.

Another important step in my Christian life was realising that my story is not just a story about Rita Nightingale who was in prison and who was set free by a miraculous pardon. It is a message for everybody. As I had to come to terms with being an ordinary person, attending a local church, helping to nurse my Mum in her sickness, I saw the same

---

1. Words and music by David Rees, from The Mighty Flyers, *Low Flying Angels* (Word UK, 1974).

God who had come to me in prison going out to all sorts of people, to where they were, answering their needs. So when I stand on a platform and tell what God has done in my life I am telling what God can do in anybody's life.

I have come to see the Christian life as a series of steps, in which it is all too possible to step back as well as forward. When I began to work with prisoners I was distressed to see how many who profess conversion do fall back when they are released, or even when they are still in prison. I used to feel a great burden for such people, and I would pray, *Lord, why is it that so many go back?* I used to be angry at the church because it wasn't there, helping to keep these people close to the Lord; but since then I have realised how hard it is for many churchgoers to relate to prisoners, either in prison or when they are released. How easy it is, when introduced to somebody who you know to have been in prison, to stand back, and to allow that involuntary expression to cross your face which tells the ex-prisoner, *I have decided that you are different from ordinary people* . . . It is to help people overcome such prejudices that Prison Christian Fellowship exists.

I have learned not to be too swift to say of somebody who has gone back to prison, 'Ah! His conversion wasn't real . . . She was only playing at being a Christian . . . His faith was psychological . . . She wanted sympathy . . .' Many whom I have known as radiant Christians in prison have been back inside months after their release, convicted of some crime that we had thought they had given up for ever. But God doesn't write us off. He teaches us through the bad times as well as the good. And which of us knows the pressures that an alchoholic, a compulsive gambler, a violent man, a quick-tempered woman have to bear? Only the Lord knows how strongly or otherwise we would come through stress and tensions if we had such handicaps. Ministering to prisoners, I have learned a little about being slow to judge others.

And each day I have learned more about the goodness of God. Looking back on it all – on my life before I was sent to prison, my experiences in Lard Yao, and from my release to the present moment – I am constantly amazed at his goodness.

Sometimes I am in the middle of some mundane piece of housework, and I stop and think: *Lord, you are so wonderful!* When I say that, I'm not thinking of material things, even though he has given me all I need and more. I'm thinking rather of the love that surrounds me. I think of Trevor's love, and Ben's, and that of the people all around me who love me. It strikes me as freshly as ever, how God has brought me from prison and my life before. And I give thanks.

Often I find myself smiling. The life I lead now would have appeared to me, when I was eighteen, as the one situation I didn't want. I had no idea what I expected from life then, but I knew for sure that I didn't want marriage, home and children. It was boring, it was what everyone else had, and I didn't want it. Even without the 'religious bit' I would have hated the idea of becoming what I now am.

And yet God has led me in a huge circle. I live in a house in Rishton, nor far from Blackburn. My husband is not only a local Blackburn man, but somebody I was at school with. Since Ben was born I have had to reorganise my diary, and now I spend much of my time at home with my family. What God has for us in the future I do not know, and I'm happy to wait until he shows us. In the meantime, life is so rich and busy that I have no time to do anything but live one day at a time.

God has taught me that it doesn't matter where you are or what you are, as long as you are in the place where he wants you. He loves us so much that he has a plan for each of us which, if we trust him, will give us the richest, most wonderful life that it is possible to live.

In the glamorous nightclubs of Hong Kong, I discovered that you can be miserable even when you have all the material things you ever wanted.

In the prison cells of Lard Yao, God showed me that you do not need liberty in order to have real freedom. In prisons in England I have seen Christians who are finding exactly the same thing. A prisoner wrote me recently and said, 'God has not taken away the walls – but he has certainly taken away the roof.'

He has taught me that he is above all a God of love, for whom no walls of pride or selfishness, nor of prison stone, are a barrier.

When I was a teenager I would have considered Christianity to be a system of restrictions. But the Lord Jesus has given me freedom. He has not only freed me from Lard Yao, he has freed me from myself. He has made me into a new person, still with much to learn and much to discover.

In his love, I am free – for ever.

20: Postscript

We are still having good Bible Study groups. The Thai group has really grown. They are still meeting in the library with about 78 in attendance.

Letter from Gladys Martin in Bangkok, June 1983.

I continue to get news of Lard Yao, from Linda and Mary and others, like Lucille and the Martins, with whom I keep up a regular correspondence.

They say that the prison has changed dramatically from what it was like when I was there. I was part of a very small group of foreign prisoners. Now there are at least forty foreign women, half of whom are serving ten, fifteen or twenty year sentences. The prison kitchen, where I spent many happy hours with Hannah baking food for the shop, has now been transformed into a highly efficient food factory with a gleaming new oven. It turns out innumerable loaves of bread and fancy cakes every week. There isn't leisure now for the privileged foreign prisoners who work there to take a late breakfast in the interlude between bakings.

While Jenny was still inside I sent her a parcel with some things she'd asked for – skirts, T-shirts, cosmetics, things like that – and in her letter back she told me that I wouldn't recognise the place. Uniforms are now compulsory; you wear a particular colour to indicate what crime you have been sentenced for.

Jack and Gladys' work in Lard Yao has been growing steadily. The Thai group has seen a large increase in numbers, and some of the foreign prisoners have become Christians.

Lucille is in poor health, but is able to keep going. Characteristically, she is busier now than she ever was. Margaret Cole too refuses to allow advancing years to slow her down. 'I'm a very busy 77-year old who hasn't yet realised that the years have made her old' – last summer, she wrote to me and told me that she had spoken twenty-one times during June; she had found herself speaking at old peoples' convalescent homes and pitying the residents because they were so elderly – in fact, she was often the oldest person present!

Linda and Mary continue to wait for the machinery of international prisoner exchange to deal with their cases. They have had several disappointments, and have often asked for special prayer as they try to get on with day-to-day living in Lard Yao and try not to think too hard about going out.

I am still enjoying spending a great deal more time at home now that Trevor and I are parents. After the hectic last few weeks before I went on maternity leave from Prison Christian Fellowship, it is lovely to be with my family for most of the week. Ben is a happy, active little baby who is adapting well to accompanying me as I travel about. I have begun to accept some speaking invitations again, mainly those near to my home, but it is still too early to make decisions for the future.

Prison Christian Fellowship is changing, as all organisations do, and we are now seeing many instances of the Lord continuing to bring to fruition the things we were praying for in the lives of prisoners and churches only a few short years ago. In this book I have described the situation as it was then. For more information about the Fellowship's current programme and projects, write to:

Prison Fellowship England and Wales
PO Box 263
London SW1.

Even after several years of working in prisons I still find it difficult to give an answer to the question that is often asked: 'What do you think about prisons as punishment?'

I have to admit that I believe that many people now in prison ought not to be there. I am sure that most of them need to be punished and many have done wicked things, but punishment by putting people behind bars is to me a terribly negative act. I like the American word 'penitentiary', which expresses the concept of prison as a place where offenders are put for penance – the punishment is the fact that you have been taken out of society and imprisoned (sadly, the reality in American prisons is often far from the ideal).

But today much of the punishment which offenders receive is punishment by the internal prison system, or by other prisoners, especially in the case of young offenders who fall into a pattern of life which too easily degrades and brutalises prisoners. I believe that prison is intended to make people good; but it all too often simply makes them bad. It might seem idealistic, but for the Christian such a view is intensely realistic. Jesus came to set the prisoners free, to make men fully human, and to put an end to sin and crime. He died to make us good. Many people have served prison sentences and in the process found that to be wonderfully true.

Freed For Life

A Summary

Bitten by the travel bug, I left my home in Blackburn, England, and travelled the world. After my marriage broke up in Australia I eventually became a night-club hostess in Hong Kong. There I fell in love with James, a young Chinese man who was handsome and rich. I didn't know that he and his friends were international drug dealers.

In 1977 we were going to visit Europe. He sent me on ahead via Bangkok, escorted by a mutual acquaintance, who took charge of my baggage. At Bangkok Airport the customs officials searched my cases and found 3.3 kilos of heroin hidden in false bottoms and secret compartments.

Angry and bewildered, I was arrested and detained in police custody, then sent to Lard Yao women's prison to await sentencing under the rules of Thai legal procedure. I was represented by a Bangkok firm of lawyers, to whom I was aggressively hostile at first, as indeed I was to everyone who tried to help me and the prison officials.

News of my arrest attracted world-wide publicity. I protested my innocence, and my lawyers advised me that even were I innocent it would be better to plead guilty as that would lead to a lighter sentence.

In prison I developed friendships with the few non-Thai prisoners – I was contemptuous of anything to do with the Thai people. Hannah was in charge of the kitchens and made me face up to the realities of being in prison. Maria was a middle-aged Spanish lady. Others – Jenny, Chris, Linda, Mary and several more – were in prison for various offences and had different sentences.

Missionaries (Jack and Gladys Martin) were allowed into

the prison, but I was bitterly hostile towards them. I hated prison and was appalled by the drug addicts, the violence and lesbianism. I raged at God, the authorities, James, and everybody. My mother was flown to Bangkok by our local newspaper but she found me angry and resentful.

Two Christians – Lucille and Margaret – read about me in the Bangkok newspapers and came to prison to see me. I rejected their friendship and accepted only their gifts of food. Undeterred, they continued to visit and to pray for me. Unknown to me, many Christians were already praying for me as well.

It was the visit of Martha Livesey, an elderly lady from Blackburn who was in Bangkok at that time, that was the turning point. She left me some food and a tract. Seeing somebody from Blackburn made me break down emotionally, and I found myself reading the tract. I became a Christian that day.

A very short time later I was called to court and heard my sentence. I had pleaded 'not guilty', and my sentence was twenty years – half what had been predicted. I am sure that this verdict reflected the enormous efforts of my lawyers, the massive press coverage of my case in Britain and abroad, and the prayers of thousands of Christians. News of my conversion had spread widely, and prayer-chains were set up in places as far apart as Australia and New York.

In *Freed for Life*, I have told of the good times and the bad times in Lard Yao over the three years that passed before my release. I grew as a Christian, some girls became Christians, and we even began a small prayer group. My letters home changed from bitter and violent epistles, and I began to be able to master my frustration and anger. I began to learn how to forgive, and I began to ask others to forgive me. Towards the end of the three years a visitor, Kathryn Grant, was allowed in to see me. She had been asked to go to the prison by Chuck Colson. His ministry – "Prison Fellowship" – struck an immediate chord in me. Since becoming a Christian I had had a tremendous burden for people in prisons all over the world, and I was thrilled to hear Kathryn's stories of what was happening.

The legal battles and appeals went on and on. Each year prisoners were released under the King's birthday amnesty, but my name was not among them. I alternated between buoyant confidence that God would support me through the next seventeen years, and despair that I wouldn't be able to survive. God taught me innumerable lessons during that time. Then in January 1980 I heard the incredible news that the King had granted me a royal pardon. This was almost unheard of in Thai legal history.

I was released and returned to London, where my Uncle George met me at the airport.

RELEASE
The Miracle of the Siberian Seven

Timothy Chmykhalov with Danny Smith

The plight of the 'Siberian Seven' attracted widespread publicity and support.

Timothy Chmykhalov, youngest member of the seven, vividly recounts the events leading to the entry into the US Embassy in 1978, the long years of hoping and waiting, the uncertainty which faced them when they left in 1983 and finally the freedom which they found in America.

Release is a powerful testimony of faith and courage amidst intense pressure and threat of persecution. A story of hope and determination in the face of much discouragement.

OUT OF THE MELTING POT

Bob Gordon

Faith does not operate in a vacuum, it operates in human lives. God wants your life to be a crucible of faith.

Bob Gordon draws together Biblical principles and personal experience to provide valuable insights into this key area. Particular reference is made to the lessons he leant recently as God provided £600,000 to buy Roffey Place Christian Training Centre.

Out of the Melting Pot is Bob Gordon's powerful testimony to the work of God today and a profound challenge to shallow views of faith.